To John

Enjoy Our Local
Heritage

Best Wishes

Len Snow

June 2004

WILLESDEN PAST

Willesden Borough's Coat of Arms

WILLESDEN PAST

Len Snow

Phillimore

1994

Published by
PHILLIMORE & CO. LTD.,
Shopwyke Manor Barn, Chichester, Sussex

ISBN 0 85033 903 0

Printed and bound in Great Britain by
BIDDLES LTD.
Guildford, Surrey

Contents

To my late sister, Rena, who was born in Willesden and who would so much have enjoyed this book.

List of Illustrations

Frontispiece: Borough Coat of Arms

Acknowledgements

The majority of the illustrations come from the the superb collection in the Brent Community History Library and Archive (at Cricklewood Library). I wish to record my thanks to the untiring and indefatigable archivist, Adam Spencer, and his colleagues there. Also to Finbarr Whooley, the Grange Museum curator and the staff there, past and present (including Val, Judith, Bridget, Keith, Nick and Nina) for their willing help, resourceful assistance and unflagging enthusiasm for local history.

Other credits: The Warden and Fellows, All Souls' College, Oxford, 9, 10; Author, 91, 106; William Blackwood and Sons, 16; Brent Symphony Orchestra, 113; Harper, Collins and Co, 51; Greater London Records Office, 14; Guildhall Library, London, 13; Arthur Guinness and Co. Ltd., 128; Heinz Co. Ltd., 120, 124; Mr. John Hockey, 146; London Transport Museum and Library, 101, 102, 104; Museum of London, 27; The late Des Mitchell, 83; Mr. E. Monk, 137; By permission of the Warden and Fellows, New College, Oxford, 7; J. Pitman and Co. Ltd., 1; Phillimore and Co. Ltd., 2; St Mary's church, Willesden, 8; St Paul's Cathedral (Guildhall Library), 4; J. Souster, 30, 32, 35, 54, 90, 96, 110, 118, 121; Willesden County school, 134; London Borough of Brent, Frontispiece, 147.

My other thanks are due to members of Willesden History Society, especially Gwen Molloy, who willingly provided the introduction as well as notes on public houses, and the late Ivor Davies; and to earlier writers on Willesden's history including D. Lysons, J. N. Brewer, F. A. Wood, Stanley Ball, B. C. Dexter, F. Hitchin-Kemp, Vera Leff and, above all, Simeon Potter.

I have again enjoyed a happy relationship with my publishers, Messrs. Phillimore and Co. Ltd, particularly Noel Osborne, Helen Chadwick, Nicola Willmot and Val White.

My special thanks are always, but happily, due to my wife Joan and to Susan and Ralph for help and encouragement at all times.

Preface

Willesden maintained its individual existence as a district inside the former shire (and later County) of Middlesex for over a thousand years. It survived, independently, partly because it had identifiable borders which stood out clearly when you stood on Willesden soil. These were the river Brent (on the west), Watling Street (or the Edgware Road, on the east) and the Harrow Road (for at least part of the southern boundary). It also had, until the middle of this century, the tacit support of St Paul's Cathedral and All Soul's College, Oxford, who between them owned a large part of Willesden. No wonder it fought hard to remain in being when the London Government Act of 1963 proposed it merge with Wembley (as did the latter district, for somewhat different reasons).

Its history is concerned with the people, perhaps three or four hundred at first, swelling to 175, 000 who lived here—in Saxon times, in the Tudor period, in the 19th century, or in recent years. Many of the dwellings they lived in have disappeared as development, modernisation or simply lack of money have decreed that buildings like Brondesbury Manor House or Mapesbury or Roundwood House should be pulled down.

It has been said that history is the best weapon with which to defend the future— I agree very much with that view.

LEN SNOW
1994

Introduction

Since Simeon Potter's *Story of Willesden*, written for the Borough's schoolchildren in the 1920s and Dr. Leff's *The Willesden Story*, a social history of post-war social services in the Borough, there has been no general local history and this book is the natural successor to the author's *Brent: A Pictorial History*.

Local history is now the subject of growing interest, beyond that of the professional local historian, by residents past and present and, it is hoped, by those students who come to it via the National Curriculum.

Beneath the Borough's unpromising and often unattractive exterior, which does not, at first sight, appear to offer the fertile field for study in more attractive areas, lies a long history pre-dating Roman times; from rural scene to industrial estate; from sparsely populated hamlets to inner city suburb and the garden estate. Willesden was fortunate in having an early Chairman of the Local Board and a Town Clerk, both with foresight to preserve the many records which now provide the nucleus of Willesden's archive.

Len Snow is well qualified to compile this history; he has lived in the area virtually all his life; he was educated at the local Kilburn Grammar School and as a Councillor for 27 years he has a deep knowledge of its recent past. In covering all these aspects of local life and all those currents which have flowed here for hundreds of years, he is giving the reader an appreciation and better understanding of that part of the present Borough of Brent, once the Borough of Willesden.

GWEN MOLLOY,
WILLESDEN HISTORY SOCIETY
1994

Chapter 1

The Beginnings

Let us start, quite literally, with bedrock under London. The London basin rests on old Devonian rock. A boring, at the White Heather Laundry in Willesden, made some years ago, reached the amazing depth of 2,000 ft., passing through the chalk rim of the London basin, gault clay and 902 ft. of Devonian rock.

The river Brent has always been Willesden's western boundary. The valley, in places half a mile or more across, contained a sluggish, meandering watercourse little used for water-borne traffic. The valley bottom was understandably marshy. Some evidence of this was found in 1983 in an archaeological dig near St Mary's church.The river frequently overflowed, flooding the fields nearby.

On either side of the Brent, we have the time-washed hills—Dollis Hill and Wakeman's Hill (the highest point in Brent at 302 ft.). Across southern Willesden runs the Brondesbury Ridge with a small peak at Mount Pleasant (by a few feet compared with Dollis Hill it is the highest point in Willesden). On the eastern end of the ridge stood the windmill at Shoot-up-Hill, beyond which it becomes part of the Hampstead Heights.

The earliest sparse evidence of man's settlement in Brent was revealed by the finding of cinerary or burnt burial urns during work on the Welsh Harp in the 1880s. This was the 'Beaker folk' (New Stone Age) period edging into the Bronze Age (1600 to 500 BC). Bronze Age axes were found at Lower Place and a Stone Age flint at Neasden—the former are in the Museum of London.

Did Julius Caesar ever march through Willesden? We cannot suppose that Caesar himself trod Willesden soil, but some Roman troops may have visited British villages or farms somewhere in Willesden.

As the Romans tightened their grip on Britain, their swiftly moving legions needed roads to traverse the territory. One of the main arteries they constructed was what was later called Watling Street. It runs straight as a die from Marble Arch to Brockley Hill (Sulloniacae) and then on to St Albans and the north-west. It is the present day Kilburn High Road and Edgware Road. Its name derives from the ancient patrons of handicraft in Scandinavian mythology. Watling streets were said to be their paved ways.

According to Potter it was 24ft. wide with paving of 'large brown flints weighing four to seven pounds on a bed of reddish-brown gravel

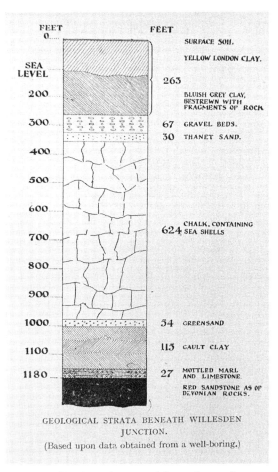

GEOLOGICAL STRATA BENEATH WILLESDEN JUNCTION.
(Based upon data obtained from a well-boring.)

1.   Willesden—the ground beneath our feet.

1

of varying thickness covered by walls of gravel-concrete which has been hardened into rock by time.'

Watling Street has been a Willesden boundary for many years. For a short period, in Saxon times during the reign of King Alfred who fought the Danes and Vikings, Watling Street was actually the boundary between the English and Danish-held land—the Danelaw. Willesden was frontier territory and this probably helped limit any expansion of the village to the east. The centre remained Willesden Green and its western outpost at Crouch (i.e. Crux meaning cross, and thereby church) End was where the church of St Mary was later established. 'The scarcity of early Saxon relics in our district (i.e. Middlesex) is best accounted for by the scarcity of early Saxons', wrote Vulliamy.

Willesden's name (in various spellings such as Wilsdon, Wellesdune or Willesdone—the present spelling was adopted by the London and Birmingham Railway when they opened a station in 1844-8—is first recorded in AD 939. The reference is found in a somewhat dubious charter associated with King Athelstan, grandson of King Alfred (hence Athelstan Gardens). Some authorities take it to be 'Hill of the spring'—Wiell meaning spring and dun meaning hill; others (including Potter) refer to the farm (tun) of Will(iam). I prefer the former origin, with Mount Pleasant as the hill, the spring going down to Willesden Green.

Most other village names in Willesden are of Saxon derivation. Harlesden comes from Heorowulf's Tun (Herewulf's or Warwolf's farm); later, a common form of the name was Holsdon.

Anglo Saxon England, under King Alfred, prospered. The shire (or share) system of government sprang up, controlled by shire-reeves i.e. sheriffs. Within the shires were the hundreds.

Willesden was in the shire of Middlesex and in Ossulstone Hundred (Oswulf's Stone) which met at Tyburn near Marble Arch where the Stone used to stand.

The monthly hundred-moot (meeting), presided over by the Hundred Reeve or Bailiff, was the place to solve local land arguments or to agree the work pattern in the fields. It was an early forerunner of local assizes, with an embryonic jury system since the number of members was often fixed at twelve. It was also local government in a primitive form, although it had no tax-collecting powers.

King Alfred's grandson, Athelstan, in that dubious charter of AD 939, granted (or rather renewed and restored) to the monastery of St Erconwald (later St Paul's cathedral) 10 manses or manors 'ad Neosdune cum Wellesdune'. These were identified as Oxgate, Neasden, Mapesbury, Brondesbury, Willesden, East and West Twyford (i.e. in the Willesden Territory though originally in the Gore Hundred), Harlesden, Chamberlayne Wood and what subsequently was called Rectory Manor. This is the view of F. A. Wood, the Willesden historian, whose transcription of old records in his own handwriting in over fifty volumes is held in the Grange Museum. This proliferation of manors and their manor houses is reflected in some of the street names—Manor House Drive from Brondesbury; Manor Park Road from Harlesden.

Chapter 2

The Norman Connections

The total survey of England compiled in 1086 and known as Domesday Book—by analogy from the Day of Judgment—was one of William the Conqueror's greatest achievements.

The full entries for Willesden, Twyford and Harlesden reveal an area of about 2,800 acres (24 hides). Since Willesden parish together with East and West Twyford comprise about 5,000 acres, it leaves much wasteland, marsh and common-land not identified with any particular ownership and not fit for cultivation.

The Canons of St. Paul's hold WILLESDEN. It always answered for 15 hides. Land for 15 ploughs. The villagers, 8 ploughs; 7 possible.
25 villagers; 5 smallholders.
Woodland, 500 pigs.
Total value £6 6s 6d; when acquired the same; before 1066 £12.
The villagers hold this manor for the Canons' revenue. Nothing is held in lordship; the manor was for their household supplies before 1066.

The Canons hold HARLESDEN as one manor*. It answers* for 5 hides. Land for 4 ploughs. In lordship 2 ploughs. The villagers, ½ plough; 1½ ploughs possible.
12 villagers with 1 virgate each; 10 villagers with ½ virgate each.
Woodland, 100 pigs.
In total, value 35s; when acquired the same; before 1066 £4.
This manor was in the lordship of the Canons of St. Paul's before 1066 and still is.

---

2. Willesden and Harlesden in Domesday Book.

The two Twyford hamlets (the western eventually went into Ealing) were both held by St Paul's cathedral and together had about 37 people. The highest value in the area was in the small Twyford manor at 15 shillings each hide—maybe a reflection of the rich pastures along the lush Brent valley. The area is now railway sidings and what was until recently the Twyford tip, which a widening of the North Circular Road has removed.

Willesden manor was in the centre of the parish and was estimated at 15 hides or about 800 acres. Harlesden was about 5 hides and both were under the jurisdiction of St Paul's. They had some 120 and 90 inhabitants respectively. The only recorded mill in the area was, presumably, a water mill by the Brent probably near the Neasden bridge.

The Church

It is claimed that St Mary's church was founded about AD 939, maybe by some association with the granting of the supposed charter by King Athelstan. Possibly a wooden structure existed in Saxon times, though no traces have been found. A Norman font and the remains of a Norman window are 12th century; the main part of the building dates from the 14th century.

The church stood among trees, surrounded by a belt of commons stretching across the parish from the Brent on the north to Harlesden on the south. This belt, which divided at Neasden, with Dudden Hill Common on the east and the Brent marshes on the west, left the church on an island surrounded by great trees. This island has always had the name of Church End partly because it was situated at the end of the road which formed communications with London and the outer world. It must have presented a charming rural picture in those days, quite impossible to visualise from its drab surroundings of the present time.

The sound of bells summoning the communicants was, perhaps, the only loud sound to crack the tranquillity of the rural air. As Simeon Potter wrote, 'they are the poor man's music'.

At some time in the 14th century, the shrine of the Virgin Mary ('the Black Virgin of Willesden') became renowned as a place of pilgrimage due to the miraculous powers ascribed to the statue. It was destroyed in 1538 during and because of the Reformation. The shrine was restored in 1952 to the Roman Catholic church in Nicoll Road; a new statue to the Black Virgin is in St Mary's itself.

A parish priest was recorded at St Mary's in 1181 (Potter): 'The church of Willesdone is in the possession of the canons [i.e. of St Paul's] and renders to them 8 marks by the hand of German the priest and pays 13 pence as synodals [payment on the visitation of the bishop].'

John, son of German, is the first recorded vicar. Willesden church appears to have had a measure

3.   Early drawing of the parish church of St Mary's, *c*.1750.

4.   Manorial records from the 17th-century survey of Prebend of Willesdon or 'Bounds'.

of modest prosperity about the date of its first major building in the 14th century, according to lists of furniture and vessels recorded after visitations in 1249 and 1297. However, a century later, the parishioners submitted a petition complaining of the ruinous state of the chancel (for which the Dean and Chapter of St Paul's were responsible). It is possible that the ravages of the Black Death in 1349 among the villagers could have contributed in some way to this decay. They would appear to have had some success with the petition since the chancel seems to have been rebuilt shortly after its submission.

The Manors

The Moot, or the Manor Court, or the Church each had responsibilities for aspects of control over the local community. There might be a constable (with a variety of duties as specified locally from looking after the stocks, inspecting alehouses and removing beggars to caring for the parish bull), a pindar (or pound-keeper to look after stray cattle or sheep (as at Pound Lane), a hayward (to look after the hay—Little Boy Blue was a hayward), an ale-conner (to test the strength of home-brewed beer) and church-wardens.

Manorial court records are a valuable source of information about this period, where they are still extant, and provide a fascinating insight into local life. Within Willesden, the St Paul's court acted in a manorial capacity and a few extracts will show how it worked.

Oct 1355   John Wynter claims to hold of the lord certain lands in Willesdon which he had of the demesne of John Markeley which formerly belonged to John Wypheley by a rent of 13s. 4d and he does fealty [this entry is dated "Court of Johannis atte Wyke held Monday after St. Michael's 1 Henry II].

               Thomas White destroys the lord's wood with his cattle: in mercy 3s.4d.

1457   John Careley, a farmer of Harleston [Harlesden] together with John and William Barnfile [or Barnaville] receives the lease of the manors of Harleston and Willesdon from All Souls College

Other local records reveal criminal proceedings for petty thieves, a priest fined for dicing or householders blocking neighbours' watercourses. Little different from today!

Chapter 3

The Look of the Countryside

The picture of Willesden in Domesday is of a sparsely populated countryside, with some villages and hamlets, set amid woodland which provided pannage for the pigs and occupying the higher ground above the river valleys, interspersed with waste and marsh and common fields. Our domain, 900 years ago, was a quiet secluded backwater in which lived hard-working villeins ('free' villagers) and farmworkers. This stable, unremarkable settlement of a Middlesex parish hardly changed during the next 700 years.

Plough-teams of four or eight bullocks would turn a furlong (i.e. a furrow-long) of 220 yards. The plowman homeward plods his weary way indeed.

The villagers were entitled to take from the woodland what each one could reach with a hooked pole or curved sickle, i.e. 'by hook or by crook'.

Some familiar names derive from this period. There is the Willesdon family (taking its name from the district), and the Franklins, Marshes, Paulets and, in Neasden, the Roberts and, later, the Nicoll families. These and others recur with great frequency, making a kind of local aristocracy. The Twyford family (first recorded in 1210 and probably derived from the estate of that name) gave service in all four main public offices. Robert Twyford was Overseer of the Poor in 1678; church-warden in 1684-87. Other names which recur in the 17th century are Chalkhill, Franklyn, Marsh, Wingfield, Marsh of Sherrick. A hundred years later, we find Joseph Finch, Thomas Nicoll, Edmund Franklin, William Weedon and Peter Mattan among those still giving service to the community.

5. Willesden churchyard, engraving by Geo. Cooke, 1819.

The Domesday survey suggests that there were about 250 people living in the parish. Five hundred years later this may have risen to about 900 (based on a figure of 240 communicants). These would have been small farmers and their families and servants with farm workers or smallholders living separately. A few craftsmen such as smiths and brewers (although in most homes brewing was a standard skill of housewives) would be found in the villages.

The Prebendal Manors

The Dean and Chapter of St Paul's farmed out the land in Willesden—that is, they collected the rent, using the earlier meaning of the word 'farm'. In 1150 the parish area was divided among the 10 manors. These were allocated to support eight of the prebendal stalls in St Paul's—Willesden (i.e. Willesden Green), Neasden, Oxgate, Twyford (East), Harlesden, Chamberlain Wood, Brondesbury and Mapesbury. One was allocated for the Rectory and the tenth manor, West Twyford, subsequently transferred to Ealing.

The prebendaries rarely visited their prebends and were usually cast in the rôle of absentee landlords. (A prebendary is a priest, serving in a cathedral receiving a stipend from the land-praebenda. The seats of the prebendaries can still be seen magnificently emplaced in the chancel of St Paul's cathedral.)

A small centre grew on top of **Neasden** hill (overlooking the Kingsbury crossing of the Brent) where the road along the Dollis ridge meets the road through Willesden to Kingsbury. This was Neasden Green with Catwood, the big house belonging to the Atwood family in 1195, leased from the Prebendary of Neasden (the 'C' is an intrusion).

In the area south of Neasden Green and west of Bower Lane—somewhere near the *Spotted Dog*—was Walsh garden, one of the many vanished names. There was a garden called Stokkes (? Stocks) also in the Neasden area. Another farm or house I have identified a little to the south of Neasden was variously called Ippeleigh, Ipele, Iply, Ypele and other spellings.

Curiously enough, the manor house of **Willesden** or Bounds (as it was sometimes called) was built eventually, not on or even near the Willesden or East Greens, but down in the south-east corner between Oxford Road and Cambridge Avenue; it was pulled down in 1825.

Kensal (Green) appears on record first in 1253 as Kingsholte or Kings Wood, but there is no indication of the king after whom it took its name (the mystery takes its place with Kingsbury). One

of the prebendal manors set up in 1150 was **Chamberlain Wood**. It was named from a 13th-century prebendary, Richard de Camera. There was a farm on the southern edge of the parish; in 1837 it was cut off by the London and Birmingham Railway from its lands. A handsome mansion actually called Kensal Manor House, on the site of a building once known as the Red House, became the home of the author Harrison Ainsworth (*see* Chapter 12).

At the eastern end of the Dollis ridge was the **Oxgate** Manor where the oldest secular building in the borough still stands—the Oxgate farmhouse, recently the home of the actor Mark Dignam. It was never a manor house but rather a typical English farm. There is a curious claim to local fame about Oxgate manor—at least four of its prebendaries were famous in their own right.

The best known is William of Wykeham (hence Wykeham School at Aboyne Road) who was born in 1323. His great fame rests as the creator and builder of Winchester College (whose scholars are thus called Wykehamists) and New College Oxford, both in about 1380. He is commemorated by a stained glass window in St Mary's church.

Twyford, as Domesday shows, was divided into two manors, East and West. The latter was not part of Willesden nor Wembley, but of Greenford. It has a strange little church built about 1720 and Twyford Abbey—which never was a monastic institution but a house built for Thomas Willan around an earlier farmhouse.

East Twyford's manor house (possibly moated), or farm, was at Lower Place, the Lower Place Farm of the 18th century, somewhere near the later Barrett's Green school. It was an area of a few small farms and nothing else of importance until the building of the canal, then the railway and, at the end of the last century, the workhouse which afterwards became the Central Middlesex Hospital. Richard Paine, who sold the manor to Sir Robert Lee in 1599, was 95 when he died and is commemorated by a plaque in St Mary's.

Harlesden Green stretched from the present day All Souls' church to Scott's Corner (at the junction of Wrottesley and Harlesden Roads). At one period it was a narrow strip of grass and trees on which the children played and the elders sat out in the summer talking about Crecy or Agincourt or later battles and happenings of the day. *The Royal Oak* was built on the southern side of the Green, opposite the manor house and farm—hence Manor Park Road and the *Crown* on the northern side. The 'manor' house was no more than a weatherboarded cottage tenanted by

8

6. Oxgate Farm, the oldest secular building now left in Willesden.

7. William of Wykeham, Prebend of Oxgate and founder of Winchester College and New College Oxford.

8.   Memorial to Richard Paine in St Mary's church.

the Finch family who have several memorials in St Mary's. It was probably 17th century in origin but disappeared about 1887. Other cottages lay on or near the Green—it will be remembered that Harlesden manor had nearly one hundred residents at the time of Domesday. The fields near Harlesden included Pightle (a small croft or close), Lucy's Croft, Home Mead, Knowle's Shot (a piece or share of land)—remembered in Knowles House—and Hunger Hill Common Field—now Roundwood Park.

Brondesbury and Mapesbury Manor Houses survived until well into the 20th century—I remember seeing the former building, an ivy-covered mansion in extensive grounds, before it fell under the developers' pick-axe in the 1930s and gave way to Manor House Drive.

There may have been a farmhouse in the Mapesbury area in Norman times before it received its present name, but Mapesbury's name can be clearly dated for it was taken from a well-known prelate, Walter Map. He lived from about 1140 to around 1205.

In the early 15th century, various land sales eventually led to large areas of Willesden (and Kingsbury) being acquired by Thomas Chichele. He was Archbishop of Canterbury from 1414 until his death. Born about 1362 in Higham Ferrers, Northamptonshire, receiving his education at the recently created foundation at Winchester, he had an abiding interest in scholarship. This led him to found All Souls' College, Oxford in 1443, the year of his death. The land he bought went to benefit the college; much of Willesden in the Chichele Road area and in Manor Ward (All Souls' Avenue) was owned by the College. By 1597, the College owned 418 acres scattered in Kingsbury and by 1814, 421 acres in Willesden.

Peter Malorees (or Maloure) was the Justiciar of Edward I, that is, the head of the judicial branch of the King's court. For his services, he was granted land in west London stretching from Willesden to the Thames at Chelsea. Portions of Brondesbury and Mapesbury manors went into the formation of the Manor of Malorees (whence Malorees School).

Other prominent names of the period include John Carely, who briefly owned Harlesden and Willesden Manors, but was imprisoned in the notorious Fleet prison for fraud. The Frowyck family acquired lands in Willesden (and Wembley) and among them was Sir Thomas Frowyck who became Chief Justice to Queen Elizabeth I; he died in 1506. William, the Shepherd, of Neasden, flourished in the 14th century. Richard of Willesdon may have been an ancestor of Bartholomew, Keeper of the Pipe Rolls, who was buried at St Mary's church in 1492 with a striking memorial brass as commemoration.

Kilburn Priory

Although Kilburn Priory was situated between the Edgware Road and Kilburn stream at the top of Belsize Road and thus in Hampstead, its connections with Willesden are numerous (as in Priory Park Road in Kilburn) and deserve a brief mention

In the early 12th century, Godwin (of whom virtually nothing is known) built himself a

9. Archbishop Chichele, the founder of All Souls' College, Oxford. During the 15th century he owned land in Willesden which went to benefit the college.

hermitage and chapel in a little wood on the banks of the Kule- or Kune-bourne (opinion is divided on the origin of the name. For some it is derived from Kine, i.e. cows' stream. Others prefer a derivation from someone called Cylla). He was looking for a life of solitary contemplation.

Kilburn Priory was later one of about half a dozen nunneries in and near London to which nobles, gentry and the superior ranks of burgess sent their daughters to follow a life of religion if they could not be suitably married. It achieved a modest popularity and prosperity. The building and the chapel were enlarged and dedicated to St John the Baptist. Kilburn Priory was closed during the Dissolution by Henry VIII in 1536.

The Priory was often visited by travellers who had few other places to rest and seek refreshment, for example, poor pilgrims *en route* to St Albans and Willesden. The buildings were said to be still standing in 1722 but nothing was left by 1814. Nearby, the Kilburn Wells and Tea Gardens sprang to fame.

The Waters were said to be 'good against all scorbutic humours, blotches, redness and pimples in the face, for inflammation of the eyes and all impurities of the skin'.

In the 19th century, the *Bell Inn* and *Red Lion* on Kilburn bridge grew in popularity as places of resort and the tea gardens faded with the disappearance of the supposedly health-giving waters. There is a plaque on the wall of the bank on the corner of Belsize Road to commemorate the site.

The lands of the Bishop of London, of St Paul's and of All Souls' College in Willesden and Kingsbury however remained untouched by the dissolution of the monasteries. There is a story that Thomas Cromwell (who, in connection with the Visitation of monasteries, had himself created Vicar General) sheltered at Brondesbury Manor House and might have protected Willesden from the depredations of Church property taking place elsewhere.

Chapter 4

Roads, Villages and Fields

Roads in the Middle Ages

Watling Street is the only Roman road in the area. From it went Mapes Lane (now Willesden Lane) which led on past Willesden Green to Dudding Hill. From here the lane to the church end of the parish enabled parishioners to visit the church for their various occasions. The main 'road' continued over Neasden Hill, then down, as Kingsbury Lane, to the crossing of the Brent. To the south, the Harrow Road wound its way across common

and heath, past Harlesden Green over the Brent at what was later the Stone bridge to Wembley Green.

The local landowners were expected to look after the adjacent roads. Thus the owner of Mapes House was supposed to take care of Mapes Lane (Willesden Lane); the Lord of Neasden to take care of Neasden Lane and Kingsbury Bridge. However, they were often lazy and negligent; the roads deteriorated, becoming impassable;

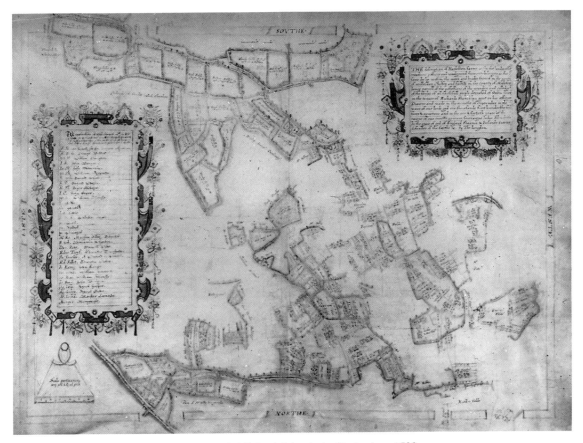

10.   Map of All Souls' lands in Harlesden, 1599.

complaints were fruitlessly made. Watling Street was, more often than not, in a poor condition.

Frequent bequests for the repair of roads are noted in records of the period. John Armstrong, 'a citizen and cook', bequeathed money for the repair of Mapes Lane in 1352. In 1415, John Robard made a grant towards the mending of Boure Lane (Bower) Lane which led off Watling Street past Coles Green and up Dollis Hill to Neasden: it is now Dollis Hill Lane.

From Harlesden Manor and the Green, Harlesden Road (earlier called Petticote Stile Lane) linked that hamlet with Willesden church. The twists and turns of the old road can still be traced near Roundwood Park and Willesden Hospital, where it ran round the boundaries of long-forgotten fields. Brands Causeway (roughly along the line of Brondesbury Park) provided the same service for Brondesbury Manor. Sherrick Green Lane (Melrose Avenue and Kendal Road) followed alongside the Slade Brook from Walm Lane to Dudding and Neasden Hills.

The Brent was crossed at three places on the Willesden border and at one other a few yards outside the boundary. The original places were Brent bridge (the Edgware Road crossing, on the border with Hendon), Kingsbury bridge at Neasden Lane, and Stonebridge under the Harrow Road. In addition there was the Silk bridge, actually in the West Hendon salient, i.e. now Barnet borough.

Hay Farms

Agricultural prosperity in the 16th and 17th centuries is reflected in the number of farmhouses which were built (or rebuilt), though in Willesden few traces remain. There is Oxgate Farm in Neasden. Mapesbury and Brondesbury Manor Houses and the Grove are other examples, though they have now gone.

The enclosure of common fields was beginning. By 1600 Harlesden was largely enclosed. Nonetheless, the essential tenor of life in Willesden remained rural and agricultural but prosperous.

Wheat was predominant in the area up to the end of the 17th century but the need for hay and meat for London brought about a gradual change. It was a precarious business because of its dependence on weather—when the hay crop failed in 1830 there were deaths among the Irish labourers at Willesden.

The All Souls' College records reveal many instances of sale of timber from their land at 'Crekyll Woddes' and from Kingsbury and Willesden during the 16th and 17th centuries.

The population of the Willesden area in 1550, based on houseling people or communicants, was between four and five hundred. This was something near double the Domesday figures—a very slow and gentle increase over 500 years. The hearth tax assessments suggest a population of about 500 in 1662.

By the end of the 18th century, the population had risen, but only slowly. In 1810 Willesden had about 130 houses (according to Lysons; 98 according to E. W. Brayley quoting from the 1801 census) with a population of between 715 to 750 (Lysons' figures).

Change was around the corner, although enclosure came later in Willesden than in many other parts of the country.

Chapter 5

Law and Order and the Settled Village

How Rates Started

It is a well-worn cliché that people pay taxes in sorrow and rates in anger. The Court of Exchequer records show that the Willesden assessment for 1331-33 was of the value of £8 11s. 8d.

The origin of local rates as we know them today is to be found in the Poor Law Act of 1601, which is regarded as the basis of the poor-rate system which lasted until 1835.

F. A. Wood tells us that, in 1662, a man, his wife and four children could not be supported on under 10s. a week. Here are some interesting examples of payments by the Willesden vestry:

1678	Paid Widd. Paine for keeping Porter's children 9 weeks	5s.
1680	Paid Mr. Ramsbrines for Widow Steele	2s. 5d.
1680	Paid Edward Freelove for bavons for ditto	16s.
1681	Paid John Feltham for keeping his mother 11 weeks at 4s.	£2.4s.

(Bavons, or bavins, are firewood)

Justices of the Peace

In Willesden, Justices of the Peace included: Thomas Niccoll of Willesden listed in 1761. One list of those who held the Commission of the Peace, written in a beautiful script, for the year 1780 set down: 'James, Duke of Chandos John St. Ledger Douglass, Wilsdon Green Joseph Gibson, Brands "nr. Willsdon"' as well as three members of the Clutterbuck family from Stanmore who had extensive interests in the licensed victualling trade.

The Middlesex Session records are full of interesting cases which hide human stories about which we are denied the full background.

The Settled Village

In 1540 Neasden was a pleasant little village atop the hill with Catwood House facing the lane which led down to Kingsbury Bridge. It had an orchard and kitchen garden at the back and Halecroft field beyond. It stood on the corner of the old loop of Bower Lane (roughly, Tanfield Avenue and part of Dollis Hill Lane). Neasden Green lay opposite Catwood (later Neasden House), with Lyttels on the south side, where later stood the Grove (now demolished) and the Grange (still with us, housing the Local History Museum which the author had the honour of opening).

The Roberts family dominated Willesden and especially Neasden in the 17th century. There was a Roberts family in the area since at least about 1390 when Ralph Roberts was appointed constable of the parish of Willesden. John Roberts seems to have been the ancestor from whom the family derived its initial wealth since it was he who bought Catwood in 1409.

Thomas Roberts, John's great-grandson, moved to Catwood and then proceeded to enlarge it, but he died in 1523. It is one of his sons, Edmund, whose brass so splendidly adorns Willesden church. The most famous of all, William Roberts, knighted at the age of 19 in 1624, was Edmund's great-grandson. The genealogy of the known Robert's members, including Williams' 10 children (three of whom were called William, two dying as infants—one can see sad Sir William hoping for a boy called by his own name to carry on the family tradition) covers many pages of F. A. Wood's marvellous holograph records. Wood tells the story that in 1628 the Vicar wrote in the parish register some derogatory remarks about Sir William's alleged meanness.

The Roberts family, particularly Sir William who became a Parliamentary supporter, profited by the death of King Charles. In 1642 a Protestation or Declaration was signed up and down the country against Charles I. Amongst a list of 159 names recorded by F. A. Wood are two Ministers, Richard Clarke and Richard Roberts, Sir William Roberts himself and other members of his family, John Finch, Edward Chalkhill, various members of the Marsh, Franklyn and Walbank families—all giving their personal signatures.

There is a tradition that Cromwell, the Lord Protector, visited Neasden House. A local builder reported that, when carrying out restoration work at the church, he found some Parliamentary bullets

11. St Mary's and the *Six Bells* in 1809—handy for the vestry to meet.

in the door. Sir William would be the most likely person to have issued the invitation. In 1649 he added to the Neasden estate the manors of Oxgate, Harlesden and Chamberlain Wood. Mapesbury and Willesden escaped his clutches and were acquired by a James Noel of London and by Ezekiel Tanner respectively. Edward Roberts sold Brondesbury Manor to Ralph Dawes in 1649 but resumed control in 1660. Yet, on the Restoration, William was back in royal favour and was created a Baronet. This was the peak of the family fortunes; gradually the Roberts' estates were disposed of to other landowners. A block of flats off Neasden Lane is named Roberts Court.

One of the most prominent of the Franklin family of Willesden was Sir John (spelt as Francklyn), who was an M.P. for Middlesex in the early 17th century and who died in 1647. There is a delightful monument in St Mary's church, lovingly erected by his wife with a charming inscription of affection and dedication—well worth looking for on a visit to the parish church.

The Marsh family begin to appear prominently—they later acquired Brondesbury and Mapesbury. The Taylors took over in Harlesden. Robert Steele and then William Godfrey came to own Chamberlain Wood. Other lands were acquired by Thomas Wingfield of

Willesden (including the Grove and the Grange) and by Richard Howe of Wokingham Place. Later, in the 18th century, Lady Sarah Salusbury (or Salisbury), the widow of Sir Thomas Salusbury, Judge of the High Court of Admiralty, acquired a large area identified with the Malorees estate. Her name is, of course, retained in Salusbury Road. Her land included the Willesden Manor with its manor house near Kilburn turnpike and parts of Brondesbury. Harlesden appears as, comparatively, the fastest growing village in Willesden, with the 'manor house' mentioned earlier. Robbins refers to an account for tiles burned at Harlesden in 1500, one of the few known examples of industrial activity in the area.

There were pounds or pens for stray cattle on Willesden Green, Neasden Green and one near Petticote Stile (hence Pound Lane) built in 1828. Mr. Kilby was pound-keeper there and was empowered to charge a fee of 4d. per animal impounded; it was still there in 1898. There was another pound in Edgware Road, that is, at the Maida Vale end of Kilburn High Road where it crosses the Kilburn stream or Ranelagh Brook.

The great plague of 1665 was the worst of a series of plagues that troubled England in the 17th century. Harrison Ainsworth's novel *Old St. Paul's* is an exciting account of the effect of the plague on London.

Chapter 6

The Ending of Rural Willesden 1800-1870

Enclosure
The law locks up both man and woman
Who steals the goose from off the common
But lets the greater felon loose
Who steals the common from the goose

(Anon)

We are all familiar with the patchwork quilt appearance of the English countryside. Take a trip to the top of Barn Hill (in North Wembley) and, looking north over playing fields and Fryent Way open space, you can get a glimpse of the farmland which was Wembley up until the 1930s and Willesden even up to the beginning of this century.

The Enclosure Act passed in 1805 changed the face of the parish in the space of a few years. Commissioners appointed in 1815 were Thomas Brown and John Sellon, and later his brother William—hence Sellon's Farm and Sellons Avenue. John Baker Sellon was a barrister, who became a magistrate in London. He was one of three sons of the minister of St James' Clerkenwell in the latter half of the 18th century. In addition to land in Harlesden, he owned a house in Pinner from 1805 to 1821.

The common fields at Dudden Hill, Hunger Hill (Roundwood), Upper Downs and the Marsh were divided up and sold. Some 560 acres were enclosed, about one-eighth of Willesden territory.

The principal landowners attested by the Award, dated 13 August 1823 (other than the Prebendaries of the Manors who were 'entitled to a proportion of all the commons and waste lands in the parish of Willesden') were the Deans and Chapters of St Paul's and of Westminster, the Duke of Buckingham (from whose courtesy title comes Chandos Road—his ancestor built Canon's Park), Thomas Nicoll and All Souls' College. They were entitled to rights of common, of pasture and other rights over and upon the commons and waste grounds.

All Souls' College came away with nearly 500 acres—about one-tenth of Willesden; the Duke of

12. John Nicoll, 1758-1819, moneyer of the Mint, one of the beneficiaries of the Enclosure Act in Neasden.

Buckingham nearly as much—452 acres, the Prebends of Brondesbury, Mapesbury, Willesden and Chamberlayne together nearly 800 acres, the Brett estates in Stonebridge 251 acres (hence Brett Road formerly called Queen's Road—also Waxlow Road after land the family owned in that area of Ealing); Thomas Willan in Twyford, Richard Taylor (Taylors Lane), Joseph Finch, 300 acres in Dollis Hill and Sherrick Green (hence Finch Close); Sir Richard Carr Glyn (hence Glynfield Road—the area was later acquired by the Earl of Craven—thus Craven Park); Robert Tubbs (Tubbs Road) and the Nicoll family, John, Joseph and Thomas

15

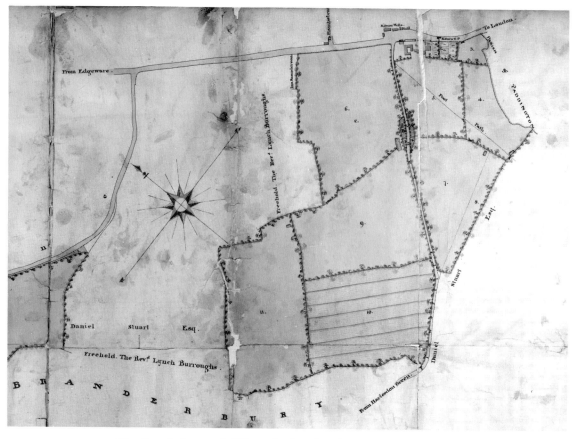

13.   Brondesbury and Kilburn lands, after the 1815 Enclosure Act.

(Nicoll Road). This is a fair catalogue of Willesden gentry and farmers—and the list of quite sizable acreages could extend to another dozen names.

Lines of old hedgerows, thought to have been obliterated by the march of buildings over Willesden's fields as described in the following pages, can still be seen, if you know where to look. This was discovered in research by Leslie Williams, the Brent Countryside Ranger in 1988-89 and documented in the *London Naturalist* (vol. 67, pp. 21-22).

Willesden Begins to Grow

In Willesden, the population, as recorded in the censuses which started in 1801, dropped slightly from 751 to 671 in 1811 but then doubled by the year 1821 to 1,413—the variation may be due to better recording procedures—Isaac Franklyn was the overseer for the third census. By 1831 it had risen again but only to 1,876 people—in each case there were slightly more females than males—and in 1841 to 2,325 people.

Brewer, in the compendious volumes *Beauties of England and Wales* of 1815, described Wilsdon (or Willesden—both spellings were used, the latter and current version being introduced for the first time that I have traced) as mostly meadow or pasture. The survey continued by describing Willesden as a 'neighbourhood more rural and tranquil than might be expected in the vicinity of London. The houses are few and, in general, widely scattered. Yet the scenery is invitingly picturesque at many points and the place would appear calculated for the retirement of the citizen, if contrast and repose be the object which he seeks in country residence.'

From the *Gentleman's Magazine* of 1822 comes this charming description of a walk to Wilsdon (reprinted in the *Willesden Guide* of 1935):

At the entrance to the village, on the left, is Brandsbury House, the elegant seat of Sir Coutts Trotter; nearly opposite, on the right, is an antique farmhouse. In a mile down the village, the Green is approached, which has

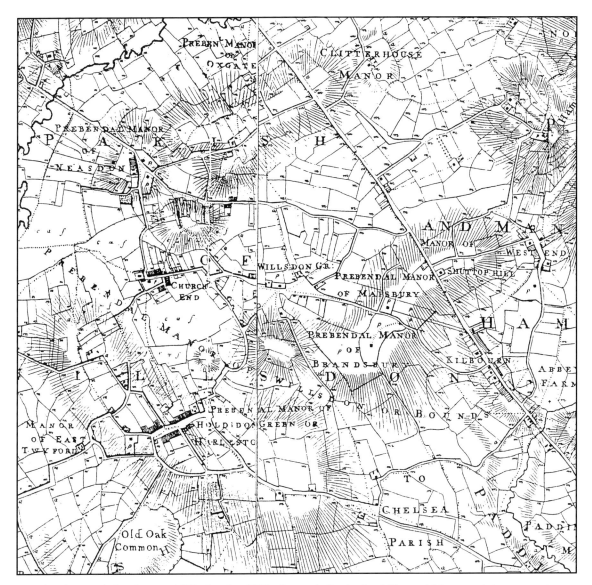

14. A map dating from *c*.1800 showing Willesden and district by Milne, widely regarded as accurate.

been partly enclosed but still retains the appearance of a sequestered spot. On the right, on Dollar's Hill, is Mr. Finch's Farm, which as an object from the valley below has a pleasing effect; but the greatest attraction is a hill on Mr. Richard's farm on the left, commanding a fine view of Windsor; and as far as Leith Hill, in Surrey.

Descending from this hill to the Green, the garden and residence of Mr. Richards is worthy of notice. At the distance of half a mile farther, at the extremity of the village, is

the church. The parsonage house, the churchyard, and an extensive prospect behind, with Harrow spire in the distance, have a most picturesque effect.

The spelling of Dollis Hill as 'Dollar's Hill' reflects the printed variation of a spoken name, otherwise shown as Daleson or Dollys Hill—possibly a personal name of a farmer whose name is not recorded elsewhere. Mr. Finch's farm was Dollis Hill Farm and some cottages still stand on Dollis Hill Lane. Mr. Richards' farm would seem to be the Grange behind Willesden library, the view being from the top of Chambers Lane.

This hint of the rustic bliss to be found in a short distance from the metropolis was reflected in small villas built on the Harrow Road at Kensal Green, on the Edgware Road at Kilburn and along Mapes Lane (Willesden Lane).

It was not always country charm. In Willesden in 1828, heavy autumn rain left the wheat crops mildewed and spoilt nearly all the hay. General distress led to outbreaks of terrorism (not many years before, there had been the Peterloo massacre in Manchester and the Luddite uprisings had taken place in the north of England). Farmers tried to help tenants protect their stacks from arsonists.

In 1840 a farm labourer earned about fifteen shillings a week (75p) on which to keep a wife and perhaps three children. Unskilled workers earnt less and could not always buy meat. By contrast, the wages for labourers 'on the parish' as recorded by the Harrow Vestry in 1834 were: man and his wife 6d. a week with a penny extra for each child—hardly a generous settlement.

In 1843 the Surveyors of Highways of St Luke's, Chelsea, met their then neighbours of Wilsden (George Hodson and William Dukinson) to agree a map showing the boundary between the parishes. They traced the line from the *Plough* in the Harrow Road—there was another inn of the same rustic name a hundred yards away in Kilburn Lane—eastwards along the centre of the latter road to a point near the *Falcon*. It was identified mainly by the trees. On the way, the cheerful band of surveyors passed Hodson's own farm. There were about thirty cottages along the west side of the lane including Regent Street (the south-east boundary along the line of the Ranelagh Brook was not decided until thirty years later).

Among the names of the 'Gentry' in *Kelly's Directory* of 1845 are Lord Decies, Mrs. Finch (at 'Dolleys Hill'), the Rev. John Gray of Whembley Park, Charles Hambro (at Brandsbury Park), Dr. John Knapp, DD, the Rector of St Marys, Colonel Knox, Joseph Nicoll (Neasden) and William Sellon. 'Traders' included Mrs. Mary Bensted, Mistress of the National School and her husband, Thomas,

15.   The *Old Spotted Dog*, Neasden, 1883. At one time the Twyford brothers ran both *Spotted Dog*s.

deputy Registrar of births and deaths, William Clary at the *Crown*, Harlesdon, George Jackman the smith at Neasden, Edmund Tattersall, farmer at Oxgate and the brothers Twyford who ran the two *Spotted Dog* inns at Willesden Green and at Neasden. The police station was at Stonebridge under the control of Sergeant William Gladman. The post office (Edward Brown) dispatched letters at 10 a.m. and 5 p.m.

There was also some development along Edgware Road including the cluster of villas known as Waterloo; in the grounds between numbers 3 and 4 was a 400 ft. well.

Several policemen, who had been recruited to the still fairly new Metropolitan Police from country districts, settled in Kilburn and married local girls.

The Desirable Suburb

In 1846 something happened of the greatest importance to the development of Willesden. The Ecclesiastical Commissioners (now the Church Commissioners) decided to review the extent of their land-holding. 'The larger portion of the Prebendal Estates possess in our opinion a [building] value far beyond their present Agricultural value'—this was a report presented in early 1847. On the Chamberlayne Wood Estate, the rising slope gave a singularly fine view extending to the Surrey hills, despite the London and Birmingham Railway cutting across its southern portion. That was where they hoped development would take place.

Between 1841-51 Willesden's population increased from 2,325 men and women (not counting 501 sleeping out, some of whom were listed as 'engaged in Smithfield Market') to 2,920. The increase was mainly in the Kilburn Lane corner of Kensal Green. The old Green was situated at the junction of Kilburn Lane and Harrow Roads.

Kensal Green was drawn out along the Harrow Road from Harrison Ainsworth's occupation of Kensal Manor House down to Kilburn Lane. It has hardly changed. The houses opposite the cemetery (opened in 1832) are the same—the cemetery wall is still there and also the *William IV* public house. There was a cluster of houses around the junction of Kilburn Lane and Harrow Road where the cemetery workers lived, including Regent Street. From there, east to Kilburn, was farm land, including George Hodson's 150-acre farm.

In the year of the Great Exhibition, the 1851 census does not reveal any significant move towards the urbanisation of Willesden despite the views and expectations of the Ecclesiastical

Commissioners and notwithstanding the easier travel facilities offered by the L.N.W. Railway which opened a station on the Edgware Road in 1852 (Kilburn High Road station).

The buildings started along the Edgware Road but none of South Kilburn itself had yet been built. The first houses in South Kilburn were at Bridge Crescent (later Bridge Street) and those were the ones which first alerted the Ecclesiastical Commissioners to what was happening. Nearby was the delightfully named 'Vale of Health'; five cottages whose residents included a bootmaker and a fishmonger.

There were only 550 persons living in Kilburn in 1851 compared with about 800 in Kensall (*sic*) Green. Along Kilburn [High] Road was a series of terraces and cottages—Felton's Cottages, Chapel Terrace, Cock Garden (a score or more of tiny cottages strung out in what had been the garden of the *Cock Tavern* opposite Quex Road). Next door to the latter was a small National school (usually known as the Cock school, originally

16.   W. H. Smith, one of the famous bookselling family, one-time First Lord of the Admiralty and the subject of satire in Gilbert and Sullivan's *H.M.S. Pinafore*.

17. Cottages in Grange Road, *c*.1910 (home of Miss Holben).

18. Harlesden Road cottages, on the site of Willesden fire station, *c*.1904.

19. Willesden fire volunteers at Chapel End (Queenstown) passing the old Sunday School, *c*.1895.

erected on the site of an old parish pond). Kilburn House, the home of W. H. Smith, the bookseller and his son, also W. H. Smith. In 1840, when he was about fifteen years old, his father bought the house; it was then described as a pleasant suburban villa standing in ample private grounds. They lived there (journeying daily to the firm's Strand offices) until 1858 on the retirement of old Mr. Smith, since by that time the area 'had become built-up'. W. H. Smith (1825-1911) went on to become an M.P., First Lord of the Admiralty and known through Gilbert and Sullivan's parody *Ruler of the Queen's Navee.*

Behind Kilburn [High] Road some fields were taken over by the Victoria Rifles for drilling and gun-shooting and for training soldiers for the Crimean War 1854-56 (hence Victoria Road). By 1868 the officer-in-charge was Adjutant-Captain Abraham Trew. There was a brewery near what is now Dyne Road, adjoining Waterloo Farm.

Willesden Green, at the time of the Enclosure Award of 1823, was some 23 acres in size. It was, at that time, split into two sections: the East Green stretched, in an irregular shape on the north side of the High Road from near the *Spotted Dog* to about the site of Willesden Green station and almost to Pheasant Lodge. The West Green began near the present police station with its western boundary along the line now occupied by Hawthorn Road and took in both sides of Harlesden Road to Grange Road and a further slice on the south side of the High Road up to Walm Lane. (The shape and size of the Greens changed from time to time.) Cottages on Harlesden Road on the Green were pulled down for the

Willesden fire station. Other cottages in Grange Road survived until the 1920s before being demolished, some to make way for a motor works and garage.

Pound Lane is identified by four cottages and 14 people. This is where the main road does a double bend between Pound Lane (the pound there until well into this century) and Dudden Hill Lane, where there was a Nonconformist chapel. By 1895, it was presided over by the Rev. Jonadab Finch, FRGS. With his delightful biblical name, he was to play a part in Willesden's affairs; meantime he was secretary of an orphans' school. The chapel which gave its name to Chapel End (also called Queenstown) is no more; built about 1820, it was pulled down in the early 1900s for a tramway widening. Opposite later, was Pendleton's corner, next to the curiously named inn, *The Case is Altered*. The hamlet had nearly 200 inhabitants, mainly farm workers and also quite a few laundresses.

Church End was a little smaller but boasted the *White Horse*, the *White Hart* and the *Six Bells*, the school and, of course, the vicar who lived in Mead House—the vicarage and rectory being leased out.

The first recorded school in the district which has persisted until today was the one attached to, and named after, St Mary's church, Willesden. It opened in 1819 when, for a penny a day, a basic education was provided in a small building near the *Six Bells*. A purpose-built school-house was provided in 1840 which remained until 1975 when it was closed in favour of a new and enlarged school to the south of the church, which was part

20. The *White Horse*, *c*.1895—in mid-century, used as a post office.

21. St Mary's Infants' School, Pound Lane, *c*.1860.

of a major council redevelopment scheme. An infants' school was opened in 1857 at the junction of Pound Lane (then known as Petticote Stile Lane) and Willesden High Road—which is still in use for a community organisation.

Cricklewood was a small village with a few houses, small and large, along Edgware Road; these included Oakland House, the home at that time of Adam Steele, an attorney, and later of George Howard who was to play a prominent part in Willesden's early local government. Also, there was the miller at Shoot-up-Hill windmill, a smith (Mrs. Jones—women's liberation started early in Willesden), an academy run by Enoch Hodgkinson and a ladies' boarding school.

Neasden was an even smaller village and the hamlets of Dolleys Hill, Oxgate and Sherrick Green together totalled 79 people.

Stonebridge was rather cut off from the rest of Willesden; it consisted of a few farms; three policemen found their homes in the village, including Sergeant William Pethers, in 1855, and an importer of foreign carpets who lived near the *Coach and Horses*, which was occupied for example in 1851 by Richard Gosdsell.

Harlesden, strung out along the Green, claimed William Sellons and James Wright, two of the well-known farmers of the district (Wright was also Clerk of the Bloomsbury County Court)— there was a baker, a cordwainer and a 'pianoforte small work maker'. By 1855 there was a cluster of shops serving the farmers—a smith and farrier, wheelwright, grocer, baker, butcher, bootmaker, seedsman and florist, with the public-houses or beer-houses at the *Royal Oak*, *Green Man* and the *Crown*. Mark Huish, the General Manager of the L.N.W.R., his wife and eight servants lived on the edge of the village in Harlesden House near to the station he had built for his own convenience. The big house was Roundwood House.

Ten Years—Slow but Steady, 1855-65

By the early 1860s, the development of South Kilburn was beginning to take off. The Edgware Road had seemed to be an impassable barrier to all save a few adventurous souls from London. Willesden (or Mapes) Lane was acquiring a few handsome villas; the rest was still green fields.

In 1860 the Hampstead Junction Railway was opened from Camden Road on the North London line to the Old Oak Common near Willesden. There was a station at Edgeware (*sic*) Road, now called Brondesbury. Another station called Kensal Green and Harlesden was sited at the Wrottesley Road bridge (well before that road came into existence) but soon was replaced by Kensal Rise

station, called Kensal Green until 1890.

Further south, off Edgware Road, were constructed the 38 houses of Alpha Terrace where farm workers, railway labourers, costers and carmen, lace-making women and sempstresses were soon living. Chichester Road, Malvern Road and Kilburn Park Road were built. Kilburn had come back to life—but it was amid complaints of dusty or muddy roads (depending on the weather), lack of drainage and sewerage and general neglect.

Near St Mary's, the parish church, where the Rev. H. W. G. Armstrong was vicar, 1854-64, lived the parish constable and sexton, Thomas Kendall. John Davies was postmaster at the post office next to the *Six Bells* about this time. (In 1843 the post-mistress was Mrs. Mulock, the mother of the novelist Maria Craik who wrote *John Halifax, Gentleman*.) Thomas Bensted was the schoolmaster at St Mary's junior school as he had been for a number of years and acted as Registrar in charge of the Willesden census—a genteel and practical way of adding to a pedagogue's modest income.

It was the Kilburn area, as we have noted, that showed the biggest change in the decade 1855-65 with most of the area north of Carlton Vale having been built or well under construction. The Kilburn Volunteer Fire Brigade had its station near Bridge Crescent where there was, handily, a police station. Coal depots were naturally to be found alongside Canterbury Road on the plain below Kilburn Bridge (that is the railway bridge, not the one over the stream lower down). The High Road (Edgware Road as it was called at this time) was extensively built up from the *Queen's Arms* to the North-London Line station at Brondesbury. A series of terraces rather than continuous housing was the style of building. Manor Terrace lay between Oxford and Cambridge Roads—the name can still be seen at the top of the cornice above no. 51. Salusbury Terrace with its shops stretched from Brondesbury Villas to Kilburn Square, while Brondesbury Terrace was where the Kilburn State cinema now defiantly stands.

The High Road was punctuated by pubs. Near the bridge was the *Rifle Volunteer*, as it was then called in deference to the Victoria Rifles. The *Victoria Tavern* was the name of the inn at the junction of Willesden Lane—correctly called a lane at that time. A brewery, owned by Messrs. Verey, stood next to Waterloo farm on which Dyne Road was built (named after Prebendary Dyne, at one time headmaster of Highgate school).

Other landmarks were the six lovely villas named Waterloo with their long gardens leading down to the main road; Stanmore Terrace, where

Foresters Hall now stands; St Paul's Lodge, the home of the vicar of the church then in Kilburn Square.

One of the houses in The Avenue (the continuation of Cavendish Road) was Stormont House, home, for a period, of W. H. G. Kingston (1814-1880), author of many once-popular but now forgotten boys' books such as *Peter the Whaler* and *The Three Midshipmen*. He is commemorated by Kingston House in the same road.

Beyond the North London Line and up Shoot-up-Hill was the Kilburn windmill—burnt down about 1863—the fire which led to the formation of the Kilburn Volunteer Fire Brigade. An eye-witness of the fire said, 'the sails were blazing and as they revolved they threw off pieces of burning material like a great Catherine wheel'.

The Ecclesiastical Commissioners went on to improve access to their estates—Chamberlayne Road linked Kilburn Lane with the new Kensal Rise station (1873). In conjunction with All Souls' College, the area was opened up with the sale of Banister's Farm for building (Bannister Road) and Mortimer Road one of the Commissioners, Sir John Mowbray, came from that Berkshire village— hence also Mowbray Road). Salusbury Road opened up the other end of Kilburn Lane to The Avenue—both roads replacing farm tracks and cattle bridges over the railways. (Queen's Park

22. Kilburn or (Mapesbury) windmill, *c*.1860, just before the disastrous fire.

station came in 1878-79.) The northern half of Kilburn Park was, by 1875, solidly built up; genteel villas in Alpha Place and Bridge Street. Behind Kilburn bridge were coal depots and also the first factory, developing quickly into a major industry of the area, the signal works of Saxby and Farmer. Saxby was an employee of L.N.W.R. who invented an automatic signalling device. He was financed by John Farmer who lived in Kilburn House (after W. H. Smith) from 1866 to 1882, when it was pulled down.

In the heart of Willesden, the growing settlement stretched from the Green, with Willesden House, the *Spotted Dog* (James Twyford, the licensee, was also the enumerator for the 1861 census in the area) and a beer-shop, the *Running Horse*.

On the south side, the Grange—hence Grange Road (where the library stands). From the east of the Green, the country lanes would take one to Cricklewood passing Pheasantfield, the home of R. S. Wright, and on by a footpath (Chichele Road not yet thought of) to Cricklewood House and the *Crown*.

Another Twyford, George, ran the other *Spotted Dog* at Neasden, opposite Neasden House where J. W. Prout, a barrister and landowner lived (hence Prout Grove). He married into one of the prominent Neasden families, the Nicolls, who had come to own much of the village, including Neasden House. Dudding Hill Farm was one of several in the charge of young farmers—Joshua East was aged 21.

Down the road, Eliza Geach, a widow, now lived with her son, sister and nine servants at Brondesbury House. John Anderson, a merchant, resided in Mapes House with his family and a collection of house servants, coachmen and grooms. In 1863, Edmund Yates, a novelist well-respected in his day, though little known today, wrote his most famous novel there—*Broken to Harness*. He wrote to a friend: 'If I had never lived at Mapesbury, I do not believe I should ever have written a novel.' Chester Foulsham later lived there, until 1915.

Outside Kilburn, Willesden was still largely agricultural. Its affairs were settled outside the parish—the poor law at Edgware and the police court at Wealdstone. Hostelries such as the *Welsh Harp* or the *Green Man* at Wembley invited the 'townees' to sample simple country pleasures. The *White Hart* in Church Road advertised its charming tea gardens while the *Coach and Horses* at Stonebridge offered 'Fishing in the Brent' which was then right outside the door. However, the usual customers were the villagers off the farms.

23.   The *White Hart*, *c*.1895—the horse-bus terminus.

Willesden in the 19th century, followed by Wembley, turned more to dairy-milk farming (like George Barham) which required a lot of grassland and hay-land. It also began to support a number of livery stables such as Tattersalls. Many dairy herds supplied much of London's milk. There were also market gardens and nurseries. Some farms were under threat—Bramley's in Willesden Green had been bought by the Conservative Land Company (one of the largest developers of Willesden) and Hodgson's and Sellon's farms were soon to fall to 'progress'. Farm wagons journeyed to town with hay and straw for the London stables, returning with loads of manure to be used on the farms. Other trips carried swill from the big West End hotels to the Willesden piggeries.

At Kensal Green the Manor House (pulled down in the 1860s) was next to the tollgate which closed soon after, in 1872. From here one could continue along the main road and over the railway (the bridge nowhere near as wide as today) and come into Harlesden passing St Mary's Terrace on the right and, on the left, the fields (to become Tubbs and Nightingale Roads) where the Oddfellows and others held fêtes. Another route was over a little bridge by Kensal Green and College Park station (as it then existed) into Green Lane (later to become Wrottesley Road). This would bring one to George Furness' Roundwood House and to Sellon's Farm, rejoining the other route by the *Royal Oak* on Harlesden Green, with its pond in front. The manor house, the Grange, still graced the village scene. A few houses and shops made up the rest of the growing hamlet which had the *Crown* (leased by Mr. Clary but shortly to be taken over by Mr. Beeson) also with its pond and a skittle ground at the western end.

Down the hill, to the north, there were a few villas and nurseries. There was St Mary's Road with the police station at the corner (the site is the recently much used and overcrowded magistrate's court—the police station itself was moved to West Ella Road in 1913) and in which also lived Oscar Claude Robson who was to become the Board's surveyor, and a dentist, Mr. J. T. Fripp. On the other side of the road were Nicoll Road and Sawyers Lane (Acton Lane), part of the fast-growing community fit to rival Kilburn.

The view northwards from the bend of Church Road, by West Ella Cottage gave a picture of a rolling land of green fields, trees and hillsides. Today the view across the valley leads the eye over the buildings to Dollis Hill and the fine building of the former Post Office Research Station. The winding lane down towards the *White Horse* passed the cottage of the road foreman. A few

24. Bramleys Farm,
c.1860, now Villiers Road
and neighbourhood.

25. Sellon's Farm in the late 19th century.

26. Old cottages in Oxgate Lane, 1905, near Oxgate Farm and Willesden Paddocks.

27. Neasden in 1818, a watercolour by W. H. Brookes.

villas (built by Mr. Todhunter to the dismay of the Rev. Wharton who saw his view up Church Road from the vicarage spoiled) provided some measure of rural bliss for worthy Victorian householders.

Near Willesden Junction station, cottages—just on the Kensington (now Hammersmith) side of the boundary and known as the railway colony—were built about 1870. On either side of Willesden Junction station there were lovely green fields in which sheep and cattle grazed; stately and shady trees including a fine row of poplars; pleasant country lanes and hedgerows and sheep tracks. However, a walk to the shops meant feeling the way, ankle deep in mud, along the unlit paths to Harlesden village, where All Souls' church was still only a little corrugated iron building built in 1858. Milk came from a neighbouring farm and water from the Water Control Column at the station.

We must not leave out Neasden, with Jackman's forge, which began in 1810 to serve the landed gentry, farmers and later the horse-breeders of the village and Neasden House still grandly dominating the hilltop where J. W. Prout was installed. The Grove was, for a number of years from about 1870, used as the Royal Canine Hospital. The ridge towards the east was farm-land derived from the Neasden and Oxgate Prebends, with Oxgate farmhouse.

Chapter 7

On the Move

Rotten Roads

The Harrow Road appears to have had two routes—the London or Harrow way via Sudbury Common, Vicar's bridge (made of wood and in the charge of the Lords of the Manors of Harrow and Ealing) and the highway through Wembley which crossed the Brent by the Stone bridge built (or rebuilt) 1660-1700. It was the subject of bequests from John Marshall (1507), Thomas Page (1512), Hugh Enystoo (1548), Henry Page (1558) and John Lyon (of Harrow School fame). In 1754 the road was said, despite these contributions, to be so bad that Harrow residents went to London through Acton. By 1800 it still took a wagon a whole day to drive from Harrow to London.

The bequest of the brewer Edward Harvist endowed the repair of the Edgware Road in 1610. (The latter's trust fund today provides also for

28. 'To the Paddington Cemetery', c.1860. The junction of Kilburn High Road and Willesden Lane; this was later the site of the *Victoria Hotel*.

charitable bequests which are now made by the local councils served by that road, including Brent.)

In 1654 the Willesden Surveyors were given powers to make a rate for the repair of highways and bridges. Among those listed in 1684 in Willesden were: John Marsh and John Field (singularly apposite names for a country district!). In each year, two other residents were appointed to this task.

The Kilburn Turnpike was instituted under an Act of 1712 by which part of the road between Tyburn and Edgware (which was one of the bad old roads, impassable for six months of the year) was improved under a local Trust. Although the width of the road was generally 40 to 50 feet, near and beyond the crossing of the Brent, it narrowed to 19 or 20 feet.

In 1722 the Willesden vestry 'resolved that the surveyors of the highways be allowed £4 for spreading gravel upon the ways'. In 1786 the surveyors published a list of payments which parishioners could make in place of their duty to work on the roads: '6s. each for owners of teams [of horses]; 8d. each for occupier of a £10 house; 6d. for a £4 house; and 4d. for every other inhabitant'. This was known as compounding and if this was not done there was an extra fine levied.

Canals and Railways

The Grand Junction Canal was built during the Napoleonic wars and ran from the Midlands to Brentford. It included a branch to Paddington which passed through Alperton, across the Brent valley, along the southern edge of Willesden and on to Praed Street with a link to the Regent's Canal. The *Grand Junction Arms* on Acton Lane is a reminder of the origin of the canal. A few families settled on the banks of the waterways in Lower Place. There is a delightfully imaginative description of the early days of the canals in Willesden in Potter (pp. 147-48). The life of the canal was short—railways proved the more popular mode of transport. A 'footnote' to this paragraph is taken from the Willesden

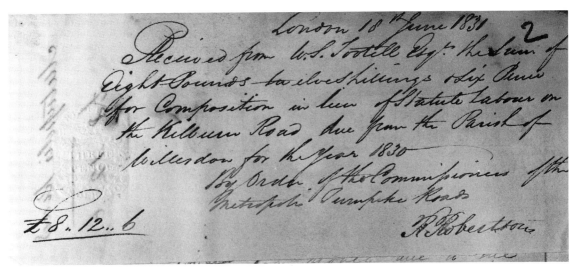

29. Receipt from William Tootell, a local government administrator in the district in the mid-19th century. For 'composition', i.e. for not undertaking road repairs.

vestry minutes of 1835: 'Resolved that the Regents Canal Co. be asked to contribute to the highway rate on account of the damage done to the roads in carrying lime and bricks to the Kingsbury Bridge' (this would be for the building of the Welsh Harp reservoir).

The Paddington branch of the Grand Junction Canal was not only used for carrying goods such as coal, road-making materials and other non-perishable items: canal boats plied daily alongside the green fields of Paddington, Harlesden and Alperton (where there is still the *Pleasure Boat* public house) to Greenford Green. Six miles for a shilling including breakfast! However, it was the commercial aspects which were more important. Brick- and tile-making at Alperton began to flourish; hay from the area was carried into London and horse dung brought back for fertiliser—recycling is not a new idea.

The canal used large quantities of water. The Ruislip Lido was constructed for its supply as the Aldenham reservoir proved insufficient. Then the waters of the Brent were tapped and a canal feeder was dug from Kingsbury to Lower Place (as the East Twyford Manor had now become). Various acts of parliament were passed to enable water supplies to be assured and between 1833 and 1835 the Brent reservoir, later the Welsh Harp, was built.

Then, in November 1840, the fields from Kingsbury to Stonebridge lay under water after torrential rain. As Potter puts it:

Still the rain continued. The worst was to follow. On the night of January 16th [1841] the dam burst and the waters swept onwards unimpeded. It was sink or swim for every creature caught that night in the oncoming flood.

There is no record of anyone being hurt nor was there any serious damage to property in Willesden itself but there was severe flooding at Brentford.

Despite their initial successes, the canals were doomed by the new monster—the railway train. More than the canal ever could, it changed the face of Willesden. It did not happen quickly but it was unstoppable. In 1830 the London and Birmingham Railway Company was incorporated. The first Bill to promote the London and Birmingham railway was defeated in 1832. The Company put up more money for compensation; the Bill was passed in 1833. In March, George Stephenson and Son, engineers (the company run by the famous railway pioneer) successfully tendered. It amounted to two and a half million pounds and the line would take seven years to build.

In Willesden opposition from landowners had slowly to be worn down. The railway entered the parish at Kilburn and progressed across the fields to the great valley of the Brent.

The long task of excavating or filling began. Fields were lost completely or cut into sections. Labourers from the navigation canals—navvies as they came to be called—bore the brunt of the back-breaking task. Many were from Ireland and more arrived a few years later as the Irish potato harvests failed. The embankment, in some parts 30-50 ft. high, edges the Brent valley each side of the great viaduct through which the North Circular Road now runs parallel to our river. The original bridge had (and still has) an arch of 60 ft. span and three land arches on each side.

The railway reached Boxmoor near Hemel Hempstead and the first section was opened on 6 July 1837. The *Visitor's Companion to Harrow-on-the-Hill* published in 1837 carried this purple patch:

> Although it must be confessed, from a mer-cantile point of view, railroads may prove of very great benefit, yet ... [we] regret that the fair face of England is to be seamed and scarred by the giant commerce and the pure atmosphere of the country contaminated by the noxious vapours necessarily arising from steam engines. In a word *(sic)* a canal may improve a landscape, but a rail-road is a decided disfiguration.

The first station out of Euston was Harrow. A station at Willesden was not opened until 1842—it was then just a few yards away from the present Harlesden station—and its purpose was the provision of a connection for Mark Huish, the ruf-fianly, buccaneering, capable general manager of the line who lived in Acton Lane. As Potter tells us, the station porter-guard-ticket-collector was known as Old Spinks and he looked after the two platforms, level crossing and the three trains a day.

The West London Railway was opened in 1844, branching off the London and Birmingham at Willesden, thus creating the first modest hint of the big junction to come. The new line crossed the Great Western lines near Mitre Junction and came to rest at Kensington (where Olympia now stands). It was a failure as a passenger railway but was used occasionally by goods trains. It revived somewhat when the extension line was built to Clapham, continued fitfully in the inter-war years especially for events at Olympia and then was discarded.

In 1846 a company with the magnificent name of the East and West India Docks and Birmingham Junction Railway was formed. It succeeded in building its line from the London and Birmingham at Hampstead Road through to Bow, thus providing a link to the City through Bow and Fenchurch Street. A line from Kew to West London Junction at Willesden in 1853 helped to create the North London Line.

Apart from the old Willesden station, the only other station in the area was Kilburn High Road. It provided the launching point for the development of Willesden.

The opening-up process was continued by the decision of the L.N.W.R. to promote the Hampstead Junction Railway from Camden Road to Old Oak Common with a spur to the main line at Harlesden. It opened on 2 January 1860 with,

30.   Willesden old station, c.1860, between the later Willesden junction and Harlesden stations.

31. Kilburn High Road with Brondesbury station bridge. The North London railway was once a possible Borough boundary!

among other stations, Edgeware *(sic)* Road at Kilburn (now Brondesbury) station.

By this time, the North London Line realised it needed its own outlet to the City and so Broad Street station (called by *Punch* the Happy Afterthought) was built, opening in 1865. With its southwestward extension direct to Richmond, the line, as we know it today, was complete. Tank engines drew 8 to 12 compartment coaches in varnished teak with red ends to the brake vans, puffing their way over embankments, through cuttings and making a swathe through the still green and bucolic districts of Willesden. The L.N.W.R. itself had thus an important link into the City. In 1865 it also opened a new train service from Euston via Kilburn to the West London Railway (at its junction at Willesden) to Kensington and then through Battersea to Waterloo and London Bridge—a version of the Outer Circle.

It could no longer be delayed! The main line from Euston to the north made some half-a-dozen junctions at a certain point 5½ miles from Euston; it was an ideal site for a station. In 1866 Willesden Junction station was born. It was a maddeningly confusing complex of high and low level platforms. It was alleged that the station was haunted by the ghosts of passengers who had died trying to find their way out. William Morris gave instructions to his daughter to avoid Willesden Junction where there were few men (i.e. station staff) and those who were there refused to answer questions. He wrote: 'The first time I went there I got into the wrong train: the second time I was so exacerbated by the coolness of the officials, that I had to offer to fight the only one I could find; fortunately for me, he refused battle.'

In 1868 the Midland Railway pushed its way from the cathedral-like terminus built by Sir George Gilbert Scott at St Pancras—one of his

32. Dudding Hill station, 1902.

earlier efforts was St John's church, Wembley—through West Hampstead to Cricklewood and Edgware, parallel with Watling Street for several miles just on the Hampstead and Hendon side. In 1875 the Midland and South Western Joint Railway opened a passenger service on the existing link line from Cricklewood through what was to become Gladstone Park at the foot of Dollis Hill on which stood Lord Aberdeen's house, the refuge of the Liberal leader. Stations were opened at Dudden Hill and Stonebridge Park (Craven Park); the line continued to Acton Wells and linked to the South Western at Kew. It contended with other routes for the title of Outer Circle but it was not successful and closed to passenger traffic in 1902, since when it has carried goods trains only.

Coaches and Horses

Regular stage-coach services began to operate. In 1681, one left Harrow for Holborn every day of the week, by 1690 another service seems to have been run by a Mr. Page.

In May 1805 the Harrow vestry recorded its opinion that a proposal to remove the two stone bridges on the turnpike road over the Brent and replace them with a new bridge between the two would be a great inconvenience to the parish.

The Enclosure Award Commissioners wrote in 1815 about the Kilburn bridge that it was of brick and stone, 37 ft. wide with the waterway beneath and six feet high. It was supposed to have been built (or rebuilt) by the Prior of Kilburn and the nuns, although later widened with bricks. The middle part was, at the time of the Award, the original stone Gothic arch.

In 1809 the House of Commons received a report recommending a general building line of 40 ft. on each side of the main roads leading out of London. The post office rejoined that a 90 ft. width would not have been too much and also urged that these roads, including the Edgware Road, be paved. John Loudon MacAdam was appointed Surveyor General but his son James did most of the work. He surveyed and improved many of the roads leading into London, including the Edgware Road.

He wrote a report on 4 April 1827 about the make-up of the Edgware Road, the widening of the

33. The *Crown* at Harlesden, 1870.

Kilburn bridge and the Harrow Road: 'which is in many parts for considerable distances, dangerously narrow and confined by high banks ... '.

In the Commissioners' Third Report in 1829, they were able to state that they had cleared out the course of the Brent where it crossed under the Harrow Road. They closed up the arches of the 'ancient bridge' to the west of the Stone bridge, erected a new one-arch bridge and restored the former course of the Brent.

In later years they flattened out the top of Hillside near the (present) police station and also Shoot-up-Hill by the windmill.

The Surveyors of Highways, by now a time-honoured office, were no better regarded than when first appointed. In 1856 the *Harrow Gazette* refers to criticisms of amateurs elected as Surveyors: '2d. has been saved to the benefit of the ratepayer for the time being but to the detriment of his comfort and to the increase of future demands on his purse.' (A statement repeated many times since!)

Although railways made little impact in Willesden until the 1860s, horse buses had been journeying, some a little intermittently, over many years. In the 1820s, coaches from the *King's Head* in Harrow left daily for London at 8 a.m. and 5 p.m. in winter, 6 p.m. in summer) and from the *Crown and Anchor* at the same times. In 1825 coaches worked from Kilburn Gate (that is the tollgate) to Bank, making five return journeys each

day. This was the period of George Shillibeer's success as a bus operator in London. R. Trevett was the operator of a similar service with 10 vehicles in 1838-39 while, in the same year, F. Meredith & Co. ran a bus from Pinner to the *Bull* in Holborn. In 1845, there was a horse-drawn bus daily to London from Church End at 'half past 8 a.m. and arriving half past 8 p.m. through Kilburn' (from *Kelly's Directory* of 1845). The coach from Harrow calls at the *Crown Inn*, Harlesden Green half past 9 a.m. and to Harrow quarter to 5 p.m. There were omnibuses to London from the *Royal Oak* at Harlesden daily at 9, 11, 2, 4, 6, 8 through Kensall *(sic)* Green.

By 1856 the London General Omnibus Company (LGOC) had been formed in Paris partly with French capital to try (unsuccessfully as it turned out) to obtain a monopoly of London buses. Among the omnibuses they did acquire were 16 on the Kilburn to London Bridge route, five plying between Kilburn and Whitechapel and three from Harlesden Green and Kensal Green to London Bridge. Monopoly or not, it was the largest bus company in the world in 1856.

A few years later, stiffer competition was to emerge—the first underground railway in the world—the Metropolitan between Paddington and Farringdon Street opened in 1863. Its impact on Willesden was not to be felt directly until an extension, some twenty years later, moved slowly but inexorably north-westwards from Baker Street.

Chapter 8

Willesden 1870-1875

Ready and Waiting

Many kinds of governing bodies existed in the mid-19th century, for example Guardians of the Poor, Improvement Commissioners, Commissioners of Sewers and Turnpike Trustees. The last-named bodies controlled the Edgware and the Harrow Road.

The harsh Poor Law Act of 1834 set up a central body of Commissioners and grouped parishes into some 700 Unions. Harrow and Willesden became constituent parts of the Hendon Union. Four elected Guardians came from Harrow and four from Willesden. There were soon complaints, certainly from Willesden, that to travel to Edgware where the Union was based was inconvenient and that the rest of the Board cared little for their problems. A salaried officer was appointed for outdoor relief. The main workhouse was at Redhill in Hendon.

Legislation to improve public health followed, including a Public Health Act of 1848 which enabled local Boards to be set up. Following an outbreak of cholera, Harrow established a Board in 1850 which included Wembley but not Willesden.

In 1870 the first and famous [Forster] Education Act was passed. The Public Health Acts of 1872 and 1875, together with the Local Government Acts of 1871, turned the minds of Willesden citizens towards the first tentative steps of local government. The fight was on for the creation of a Local Sanitary Board—an unglamorous-sounding but vital step for democracy.

Take off Point: Willesden's Fight to Rule

Rail transport, piped water and main drainage were the pre-conditions for further suburban development.

Piped water was brought to Willesden in the summer of 1855 following numerous requests from the Rev. R. W. Burton (the vicar of St Mary's from 1850-54), Mr. Vallance of Bransbury Park, a Mr. Fisher of Willesden, and others. The West Middlesex Waterworks Company had extended a

main along the Edgware Road as far as the junction with Willesden Lane (as Mapes Lane was now called). To supply Willesden, a 9-in. main was driven along the lane. A service reservoir for filtered water was completed at Donnington Road, N.W.10 in 1889, and another off Shoot-Up-Hill in Gondar Gardens in 1894. The West Middlesex Company became part of the Metropolitan Water Board in 1904. The water pipe track can be seen running across the Willesden as a gap between houses: Conduit Way takes its name from it.

The greatest proportionate increase in Willesden's population took place between 1861 and 1871—from 3,896 to 15,872, an incredible 307 per cent increase. Most of this took place in South Kilburn, which reached a crowded 10,314 inhabitants by 1871.

From the start in about 1860 on the church-owned lands fronting the Edgware Road south of Kilburn (High Road) station, the next few years saw a demonic rush to build. Kilburn Park, as the area was called (now South Kilburn or Carlton), produced some handsome three- and four-storey houses in Oxford and Cambridge Roads and less pretentious houses in a dozen roads including Alpha Place (apparently named by James Bailey the builder as the first of his developments), Alexandra Road (named in 1863 after the wife of Edward, Prince of Wales, later Edward VII—the name was subsequently changed to Princess Road), Albert Road (the connection is obvious), Denmark Road (another link with the beautiful bride of Edward who had a pub named after him in the same road). Canterbury Road and Chichester Road reflected the church connection—the Earl of Chichester was Chairman of the Estates Commission of the Ecclesiastical Commissioners. Carlton Road (later Carlton Vale), which ran through the centre of the area, was an extension of the road from Carlton Hill in St John's Wood of which district the Kilburn Park Estate was regarded as a continuation.

The people who formed the population of the teeming settlement varied—Oxford Road, for example, was bourgeois—retired Army and Naval Officers; merchants, retired or active; two surgeons; the curate of St Augustine's; a small boarding and day school at no. 32; a young actress, Helen St. Clair, and a number of widows. At the working class end of the new town, as in Chichester Road, were carpenters, painters, a gardiner *(sic)*, potmen and many labourers—none of them in agriculture. Some houses had 15 or 16 people living in them among three or four families. This was Willesden in mid-Victorian times.

Beating the Bounds

To preface the story of the fight for the Local Board, the following account of the fixing of the south-eastern boundary is retold.

The boundary between Willesden (Kilburn) and Paddington ran along the Ranelagh Brook— or at least by the 1870s memory suggested this was the ancient line of demarcation, only the Brook had been arched over and become a drain sewer. Thus, punctually, at 10.30 a.m. on Monday, 14 September 1874, a knot of persons gathered at the corner of Willesden near the *Queen's Arms* (now no.1 Kilburn High Road). They included the Willesden Overseers, Wood and Thomas, a number of other ratepayers such as Mr. Bonnett and Mr. Judd and officers, one of whom was the

ubiquitous Tootell. The parish of Paddington was represented by a smaller number of ratepayers and officers. The start was delayed a little because even at that meeting place they could not decide exactly where the Willesden/Paddington boundary lay. Once this point was agreed, the party went in single file endeavouring to trace the almost obscured course of the Ranelagh sewer. A dozen serious gentlemen in top hats and frock-coats followed the capricious stream-bed as it twisted and turned and almost disappeared after years of neglect. In one or two instances, houses had to be entered and back garden walls scaled. Some considerable time was spent in tracing the boundary at the extreme end of the parish at Park Terrace (near the Chippenham) where it was alleged there were one or two houses that had never yet been rated by either parish (in 1904 some further minor adjustments were made to the boundary at this part of the line). Passing along the back of Malvern Terrace, having left the line of the old stream, some difficulty was experienced in tracing the boundary for some reason, but it was picked up again at Kilburn Lane, thanks to the exercise carried out some twenty years earlier.

The party reached Willesden Junction where they were met by representatives of Hammersmith parish. In making the various embankments, the

34.   Looking north from the *Queen's Arms* up Kilburn High Road in 1886. Note that by now there is no tollgate.

boundary stones, which at one time served as indicators, had been removed by servants of the railway company. However, identification of the line did not prove difficult; it was agreed that the station master's house lay in Willesden.

The party eventually arrived at Mr. Clary's in Harlesden, the old *Crown*, where 13 of them, unsuperstitiously including the vicar of Willesden, the Rev. Wharton, sat down to a well-earned substantial repast. Back-slapping speeches were exchanged between the vicar and Mr. Wood who went on to recount the story of the Kilbourne.

Once the boundary had been identified with all its curves and bends, the development of Kilburn Park Road, along this line, suggested that some rationalisation was needed. For once, common sense prevailed and, at Paddington's instigation, Willesden agreed to the boundary running down the centre of that road.

The Fight Is On

The people of Kilburn were not happy, as the new *Kilburn Times* (proprietor Rowland G. Bassett, Volume III New Series, to give its own grand description) in 1869 and 1870 frequently reported. One of the big problems was the fundamental issue of the roads and the drainage.

On 7 May 1870, the *Kilburn Times*, which supported the move towards local government in Willesden, contained an editorial

> We will suppose ourselves to stand at Kilburn Gate looking northwards. The Edgware Road - upon which the original hamlet Kilborne was dropped down when all about was fields and London - a distant city - stretches behind us to Marble Arch, and before us indefinitely. Within the compass of Kilburn ... shopkeepers thrive moderately on a regular trade and an amount of flying traffic ... on the left, Oxford and Cambridge Roads terminate in the Slough of Despond we call Kilburn Park ... Kilburn has one thorough-fare, north and south. It is wide and straight, well paved and much patronised by visitors to the 'Welch Harp' and no doubt by the 600 poor pedestrians whom Mr. Wright has pictured as trudging wearily along 6 miles to answer a summons at Edgware (the Hendon Court).

Kilburn 'was born of four parishes, but no-one's child' wrote the same editor on 24 September 1870. The parishes were Willesden, Hampstead, Marylebone and Paddington which all met at the point where the present Maida Vale ends and the Kilburn High Road begins—Kilburn Tollgate; where the Kilburn stream ran under the Watling

Street and became the Ranelagh Brook (and, further on, the Bays Water).

The *Kilburn Times* reported masonry falling off a cornice in Somerset Terrace, Carlton Road, near the newspaper offices. This demonstration of the bad workmanship of some of the Kilburn buildings led to a call for the appointment of a District Surveyor. (It was five years before the cry was heeded.) Wood describes the ensuing chaos and its outcome:

> Building was commenced (about 1850) in a style and on a scale far beyond the means of the builders ... A few houses were built two or three in a road and the roads were partially made up good enough to sell the land had it been developed at once. But, as time went on, the lands became more and more divided ... Before 1865 the roads had become spoilt; houses had been built in Cambridge and Pembroke Roads, but the traffic, especially that of the builders' carts, dragging material, had completely destroyed the roadways (which were not yet metalled) and in wet weather they had become impassable ... "The [Willesden] Vestry and the Board of

35. F. A. Wood (1822-1904)—one of the founders of Willesden council.

Guardians were appealed to, but they had no power to help, nor had they any intention to interfere. The Authorities had no experience in dealing with building land ...

It was true also that no one prevented the present owners from making the best roads that could be made ... What they wanted and could do nothing without, was an Authority that could make the roads and charge the cost equitably upon the owners and such an authority did not exist in a rural parish like Willesden.

The sewers had been made with fair success, though the principal entrance of the local main was a little lower than the bed of the great Ranelagh Sewer at the point of the junction, and afterwards caused floods and other inconveniences.

As the roads were built, they were drained into the Ranelagh sewer. There was an outcry from the Metropolitan Board of Works when a developer (probably James Bailey) on the Willesden side of the Edgware Road was found to be surreptitiously joining the drains for the houses he was building in 1868 or 1869 to the Board's sewer; for this he was not liable to rates.

Agitation continued to try to force the authorities to act. The vestry refused—probably because it was still mainly composed of the 'Old Guard' from the rural villages of Willesden. The 'newcomers' in Kilburn were not so closely involved with parish affairs.

The fight was on. Meetings were held, petitions raised and polls held, from 1869 to 1873, with varying results depending on who attended or where the meeting was arranged. At one of these, the suggestion was made in a petition that the North London Line become the boundary, because of the irreconcilable differences betweeen Kilburn and Willesden. The proposition did not succeed, leaving us with one of the interesting 'ifs' of history—if Kilburn had separated from Willesden parish would we then have had the Borough of Kilburn and the Borough of Neasden?

Eventually the Local Government Board sent in an Inspector to hold a public enquiry. Samuel Tilley, a local solicitor, acted without pay and 'gallantly fought an apparently losing fight'; he was to become the first Clerk to the Board, in 1875. The Local Government Board at last decided that it was wise to give Willesden its own powers and a Sanitary Board was set up from 29 September 1874 with 15 members.

The ratepayers were then called on to decide whether or not to divide the parish into wards. The

36. George Furness, first chairman of Willesden Local Board in 1875.

sensible course was taken to create four wards, East and West Willesden; North and South Kilburn; each ward had three members except South Kilburn, the most populous, with six. Again, F.A. Wood was the moving spirit behind these proposals.

The Local Government Board approved the arrangements in December and—so speedily did they work in those otherwise leisurely days—the election took place on 22 January 1875. Of those elected, ten had been in favour of the Act including George Howard and F. A. Wood and five against, including George Furness who was, nonetheless, elected Chairman.

The arguments had been long and bitter. On the opposition side were those who feared the imposition of heavy rates. Others simply wished to keep the parish in this old-world state of picturesque seclusion—as pictured by Trollope. 'They wished to sweep at the Atlantic with mops', as Wood puts it.

On the side of the promoters were those who saw progress as inevitable. The railways were criss-crossing the parish 'like a spider's web', each stimulating new growth. The state of the roads, of water supply and the fouling of the streams and ditches by sewage, all carried an imperative argument for the need for improvement which a single authority alone could provide.

Willesden was launched irreversibly as a town in its own right.

Chapter 9

Willesden Going Places

The Local Board gets down to the job

The new Board had to create its own traditions and procedures. It took as its motto the Latin tag *Laborare est orare*—to work is to pray; it stayed with Willesden until 1965! Two members, George Howard and Charles Hodgson, prepared bye-laws for the conduct of the Council (or Standing Orders as they are now called). Meetings were held on the second and fourth Tuesdays of each month; the public were allowed to be present and the minutes were open for inspection by ratepayers—at one shilling a time. The duties of Clerk, Surveyor, Inspector of Nuisances and Collector of Rates were also laid down in meticulous detail.

The minute book (rebound and housed in the Brent Archives) starts off in the beautifully rounded script of W. A. Tootell, the Returning Officer who acted as Clerk until Sam Tilley was formally appointed. The first meeting 'at the Parish Offices, Cavendish Road' was on 3 February 1875. F. A. Wood moved that John Kershaw take the chair but, on a vote, George Furness was elected by a majority of the 14 members present out of the 15 elected.

The Board decided to pay its Clerk and its Surveyor £200 a year, the Inspector of Nuisances £100 and the Medical Officer of Health £60. The Collector of Rates was to retain two per cent of rates collected—in the first year this would have given him about £188. (Today that would amount to over three million pounds.)

In June 1875, the Board moved into its permanent offices at Hampton House at the corner of Dyne Road and Kilburn High Road, its headquarters the town hall was built opposite in Dyne Road nearly twenty years later. (A new building in Dyne Road was named Hampton House in memory of the original Council offices.)

As they got into their stride, George Furness and his colleagues divided themselves into committees—Finance (of which F. A. Wood was the first Chairman), Works (originally 'General Works and Purposes'), Sanitary, and the Outdoor Committee (a primitive environmental health

body). *Ad hoc* committees to deal with the bye-laws and with parliamentary matters were created from time to time.

The Board was responsible for street cleaning (scavenging) and watering as well as lighting (roads were dusty; hand water-carts were used to lay the dust). The 18 miles of roadways and 23 miles of footpaths were now given professional supervision in place of the amateur volunteer Surveyors of Highways.

Drainage was a major task which the new Board Surveyor, the redoubtable and expert Oscar Claude Robson, took over (he is remembered in Robson Avenue). He was a tallish man, good-looking and

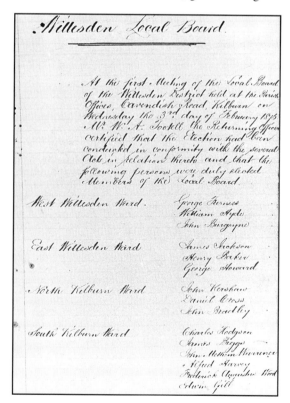

37. Willesden Board Minutes.

38. O. C. Robson, who retired in 1918 after 40 years' service as the council's surveyor.

genial to talk to. When he retired, in 1918, tributes were paid to him, including some from his 'outdoor staff'. He was regarded 'as a gentleman, a good friend, and one whose kindliest sympathy was extended to all. He was ever just and generous ... They felt they were losing one who had taken almost a fatherly interest in their well-being'. What an honour!

He was the clear-sighted officer who was responsible for establishing building controls (and for planting trees all over Willesden). All plans for development had to be submitted to the Board for approval; Robson devised a system of recording the necessary information in large, leather-covered ledgers.

One of the biggest of the property developers was the United Land Company based in Norfolk Street, Strand, which operated in the Hillside Estate, Church End, Willesden Green, Lower Place and other sites. It assembled and laid out estates in roads and plots but does not seem to have been responsible for actual building of houses.

In Harlesden, small plots were developed by local builders like E. H. Taylor who built houses in St Albans Road on the Greenhill Estate, earlier owned by Thomas Finch. Joseph Hinves and his son, builders from Rotherhithe, built in St Albans Road. Matthew and John Scott (who lived at 10 Greenhill Park Villas) built some of the houses on the corner with Nicoll Road and Greenhill Park near Sawyers Lane (Acton Lane). This was the typical pattern by which much of the development of Willesden was carried out.

George Furness, as early as November 1875, was seeking permission from the Board for drying sheds, kilns and so forth at his brickworks in Harlesden Lane and then for building eight villas on a road he proposed to build near Roundwood House along Harlesden Green Lane (which was named, later, Wrottesley Road).

In the first year, from 1 February 1875 to 31 March 1876, the Board levied two general district rates—1s. 6d. in May 1875 and 1s. in December, raising £9,697 3s. 9½d., not all of which was collected due to defaults and other reasons which have not changed in a hundred years. It should be remembered that the vestry was still levying a poor-rate which, in that year, was 1s. 6d., making a total of 4s. due from ratepayers.

The Big Show: The Great Willesden Build-Up
On 30 June 1879 the Royal Agricultural Society opened a week-long international exhibition of farming, agricultural machinery, a working dairy and everything associated with that great industry. The site was some 100 acres in Kilburn from Kensal Rise station (then called Kensal Green) on the north-west, down to the specially built Queen's Park station (then called Queen's Road and West Kilburn). The newly constructed Salusbury Road was on the eastern boundary. So big was the site that a steam tramway traversed the centre aisle. Kilburn was en fête for the occasion, although the weather, true to form, played the visitors false by raining so much beforehand that 'Exhibition' and 'mud' were synonymous in London at that time. The Society's Report on the Exhibition shows that over £3,300 was spent on sleepers and ballast to make the roadways.

The tented scene must have been a brave sight. The Prince of Wales paid four visits.

The streets of Kilburn were bedecked with flags, flowers, banners and draperies; children lined up outside the Trinity schools to sing his anthem and were warmly thanked by the royal person. Later in the week, the Queen herself lent her patronage to the show where some of her cattle competed for the many prizes. There was accommodation for 3,000 people who could not

39.   Green Lane (now Wrottesley Road), *c*.1895, showing Roundwood House Lodge in the background.

40.   The Royal Agricultural Show at Kilburn, 1879, showing milch-cows, machinery and ... mud!

only enjoy the agricultural exhibits and show pieces but take refreshments and visit a collection of ancient and modern farm implements.

The Golden Jubilee of Queen Victoria was celebrated on and around 21 June 1887 with almost excessive gaiety. Willesden erected its Jubilee Clock at Harlesden (at Cricklewood [Anson Road] there was a clock in honour of the Coronation of George V) which survives as a happy and well-maintained memorial to the imperial past. The Kilburn drapers Fisher & Co. set up a competition among domestic servants. There was a Jubilee Temperance Conference—and why not? The Local Board would not spend any money on treats, so a voluntary committee was quickly called up to provide the children with a little jollity. The inmates of the Hendon Workhouse (which served Willesden and Harrow) were allowed to have Christmas Day food on the great day.

The shopkeepers along the Edgware Road lit their shops and put up flags; every street did the same. The Board members quietly arranged a private Jubilee dinner (not on the rates) at the *Old Spotted Dog*, Neasden, where many fine speeches were made—and many fine bumpers downed! William Gladstone threw a party at Dollis Hill House on 27 May but the invitations went out late and few attended on what turned out to be a coldish day.

A few years after the Royal Agricultural Show in Kilburn, the Ecclesiastical Commissioners donated to the City of London 30 acres of the old Exhibition site to lay out as dedicated public open space. The attractively designed enclosure was opened in 1887 and, fittingly for Golden Jubilee

year, called Queen's Park. For a decade it stayed a woody enclave in the midst of open fields apart from some houses such as 'Halse Terrace' built in Salusbury Road (nos. 108-128) in 1884.

Even as late as the 1860s, Harlesden Road (earlier Willesden Lane *[sic]* and then Harlesden Lane), which wound round from the Green past Roundwood House to Willesden Green, could be described as 'almost a footpath' and the village as being 'mainly large houses and trees'. Then, suddenly, Harlesden expanded from a small country village round a green and residential roads began to appear radiating out from the village— Wendover, Tavistock, Sellons and Rucklidge Avenues (the latter named after the builder). The High Street took on the appearance which has hardly changed until today (other than the modern style of shopfronts). Above the shops were flats; the pubs; the church; and then the Jubilee Clock!

A proposal for a grand shopping arcade and theatre near the former police station in Craven Park Road at the corner of St Mary's Road was never taken beyond the 'bright idea' stage.

Party walls projecting above roof level as a fire prevention measure were encouraged by Victorian building legislation. The results can be seen for example in the houses in Dudden Hill Lane and Cooper Road, Denzil Road, Conley Road, Honeywood Road and Church Road all in N.W.10, and many others.

Apart from the small number of quite old country buildings still left standing (such as Oxgate Farm and the Grange) there are still a few farm cottages such as Stevens Cottage (behind the *Spotted Dog*) and, until recently, in Pound Lane

41. The Jubilee Clock, *c*.1895 with an unhygienic display of fresh meat at Johnson the butcher.

42.   Harlesden village in 1875.

43.   Harlesden police station, *c.*1905. The police station was situated in Craven Park Road, at the corner of St Mary's Road.

and some cottages next to Willesden vestry hall among the few farm workers' dwellings preserved by the vagaries of good fortune.

The quickening of the expansion of Willesden at Kilburn Park, Kilburn High Road, Kensal Green and Harlesden in the 1860s and 1870s was a bounty for the speculative builder. Rarely did he use an architect (for many years the standard reference book was J. C. Loudon's *Encyclopedia of Cottage, Farm and Villa Architecture*, 1833). Row after row of streets such as those between Willesden Lane and the North London Line; or between Harrow Road and Wakeman Road, the Kensal Green estate; or for that matter most of the heart of Harlesden are without front gardens. Typical streets are Earlsmead Road and Princess Road. An interesting variation can be seen just across the border at Kilburn Lane. The south side of the road down towards the Harrow Road was built by the Artisans, Labourers and General Dwellings Company in the 1880s. The design of the houses is still worth a visit.

The Brett estate in Stonebridge was also developed in the 1880s with roads northwards running down towards the canal feeder. Housing plots in 1880 were being sold at £45-50 each and shop plots at about £100. A bus started from the *Stonebridge Park Hotel* to Charing Cross to serve the residents including those of the grander villas along Stonebridge Park. The *Orange Tree* public house was built by 1883. Houses at the corners of Denton and Brett Roads bore the dates 1897 and 1899. Some of the villas remain but the rest of the estate succumbed to the redevelopment mania of the 1960s and '70s.

Another estate from this period since replaced by modern council development was on the west side of Church Road including Holly Lane, Mayo Road and Garnet Road (probably named after Field-Marshal Sir Garnet Wolseley, 1833-1913, whose exploits in the Ashanti War engendered the phrase 'All Sir Garnet' meaning everything's fine).

Willesden Green was now no longer the hamlet with the village feature its name suggests: the farms were being sold one by one—and this piecemeal process accounts for the irregular road formation on each side of the High road. To this period we owe Villiers, Chaplin and Belton Roads—built on Bramley's Farm land as well as Strode Road on the south; Huddlestone and Lechmere Roads on Willesden House grounds and Linacre Road on a corner of All Souls' land stretching up to the Metropolitan Railway. Park Avenue (Hodgson's Farm) was first named Burgoyne Road. St Paul's Avenue was, originally, Chapter Road (the western extension of this road kept the name, though it

44. Stevens Cottages, also known as the Spotted Dog Cottages until they were taken over by Thomas Stevens.

was not built until later), Dean Road and Deacon Road all bear witness to the connection between Willesesden and the Cathedral.

With these housing estates came the shops, especially along Willesden Green High Road. St Andrew's church and the police station, almost opposite each other, were built in 1887 and 1896 respectively. Despite the onward press of the brick and slate purveyors, many sites held out. At the corner of Walm Lane and Willesden Lane was 'Endlands' (later called Rose Villa), a beautiful house in its own grounds described as 'too large and elegant to be called a cottage and not grandiose enough to be considered an estate. It was like a lovely old manse, surrounded by a large old world garden back and front'—at one time in the latter part of the century it was the home of the organist of St Vedast's in the City. East of Walm Lane and 'Endlands', along Willesden Lane, there was Heathfield House, converted in the 1880s to a small, select development, Heathfield Park. Nearly opposite, at what is now the corner of Lydford Road, was Mapeshill House (no. 290 Willesden Lane). Soon it was joined by mansions like Ardagh, Longcroft, Park House and Glenmore—town houses for the gentry, some of which are still in use.

45. The chapel at Pound Lane junction remains an active church today.

Further west, next to St Andrew's church, was another, even grander house, 'Gowan Lea' (now Gowan Road—a cul-de-sac built on the old estate) and then Green Farm, still upholding the fast disappearing country traditions of Willesden. At the west end there was still the pound in Pound Lane, the old Congregational chapel on the opposite corner of the junction and then Dudding Hill or Easts' Farm (later the site of Hall's Telephones factory).

North of Willesden Green station was the large, but isolated, Pheasant Field estate. Blenheim House (Blenheim Gardens), its neighbour, looked across fields all the way to Dollis Hill.

Inside the arc of the junction made by Cricklewood Broadway and the new Chichele Road (named after Archbishop Chichele), the Oaklands Estate (Oaklands Road) was developed for housing. George Howard, its most noteworthy owner, is recalled by Howard Road (first called College Road). Rockhall Road in the same area is named after an estate on the east side of the main road, in what is now Barnet.

The 'hinterland' of Kilburn High Road was also now being built up—Christchurch Avenue and the whole area south of the North London Line and east of the Paddington cemetery, right down to the L.N.W.R. at Kilburn. Exeter Road replaced the original name of Mapesbury Avenue.

Another big development was of the Kilburn House estate, taking in much of the land between Victoria Road and Willesden Lane. The development including Glengall Road and Priory Park Road (named from Kilburn Priory). The developments came along pell mell—it is difficult to avoid making them sound like a catalogue.

Among the developers here was Solomon Barnett who lived at Restormel (no. 89 Brondesbury Road). He was one of the first Jewish names to appear in Willesden history. He fought, unsuccessfully, for a seat for the Willesden Division of the Middlesex county council in 1889. Modestly, his name is not attached to any of the local roads but Donaldson Road comes from his solicitor and Honiton, Lynton, Torbay (built on Pile's Farm) and Hartland Roads refer to his wife's home county of Devon.

The building of Kilburn Park—the southernmost tip of the district, beyond Carlton Vale—belongs to this later period; so does Allington Road alongside the railway. The circle is completed with the Kensal Green estate between Purves and Hazel Roads, named respectively after the land agent of All Souls' College and the solicitor for the ubiquitous United Land Company which developed some of the estate.

46. Dudding Hill (East's) Farm; the picture dates from between 1899-1903. Dudden Hill School may be seen in the background.

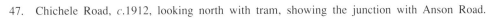

47. Chichele Road, *c*.1912, looking north with tram, showing the junction with Anson Road.

48. Kilburn High Road, north of Brondesbury station in the 1870s, before the Metropolitan railway bridge was built.

Neasden remained untouched at this time except for Lansdowne Grove (apparently built by someone who lived in Lansdowne Gardens in Brighton) and the Metropolitan Railway houses in Quainton Street already mentioned.

Among the other builders and developers involved in this massive onslaught on Willesden's farmlands were R. Bristow (Kilburn Lane and Allington Road), Thomas Spink (Fortune Gate), the Imperial Property Investment Company (Pheasantfield), G. German (Wall Road, later called Plympton Road), William Hoopell (Churchill Road and others), Mackley Brothers (Anson Road—Broadway end), George Furness (Clock Farm Estate, Cricklewood—Larch Road, &c.), Langler and Pinkham (Kensal Rise—including Langler Road) and Messrs. Rucklidge, Nicoll and Tubbs, who each gave their name to local roads. To extend this list would be tedious but the unsung 'heroes' of Willesden's development deserve a better fate than oblivion. They made Willesden according to their perception of the times in which they lived.

At this stage in our history, there was still little in the way of large scale industrial activity. One firm was Saxby and Farmer at Kilburn. George Furness built his own brickworks at Mount Pleasant, Willesden Green, to provide for his house-building activities. There was also a growing number of small workshops—smiths, wheelwrights, builders, musical instrument-makers and a host of other small businesses serving either the needs of farmers or the new town population of Kilburn. Laundries were particularly plentiful in Willesden to meet the demand from London, partly because of water supplies from artesian wells and partly because of the availability of Irish labourers' wives whose winter employment helped the family income. The building workers were underemployed during the inclement weather which, by the same token, prevented domestic households from using natural outdoor drying.

Chapter 10

Changing Willesden

The New Suburb

The dates of buildings engraved high up on houses and shops reveal the way in which the tide of bricks and tiles was engulfing southern Willesden. Stanmer House in Villiers Road, Willesden Green, is fixed at 1889—the search for evidence of construction is fascinating for those with eyes to observe the local scene. St Paul's Avenue houses are dated 1883 and 1887.

According to the anonymously written *Suburban Homes of London* of 1881:

Willesden is something more than a railway junction; it is a charming locality still, abounding in rural attractions.

The speculative builders seized their chance.

Between 1875 and 1895 over 8,000 houses were built in Willesden—at rates varying from about 350 to over 500 a year. The population increased by over 50,000 (from 18,559 to 70,403) averaging 6.5 people per new house—rather high and indicative of overcrowding in part of the Board's area. It was still one of the fastest growing districts in the whole of London. The rateable value almost quadrupled—a sure sign of prosperity.

Harlesden was still regarded as a 'tranquil and pleasant village' in which, for example, Nicoll Road, 'a handsome thoroughfare', had houses renting at £70-£80. In Stonebridge, building work was much in evidence in the early 1880s; Stonebridge Park (the road) was offering a new

49.   Willesden vicarage, *c.*1880, a typical 'country' parsonage.

50. *(Above left)* Dollis Hill House in the 1890s.

51. *(Above right)* Mr. W. E. Gladstone, visitor to Dollis Hill House in the 1880s, with his wife and host and hostess, Lord and Lady Aberdeen and Professor Henry Drummond.

60-ft. road and houses between £70 and £100. Kensal Green was regarded as the worst end and 'of the poorest character in the parish with very primitive accommodation'.

The farm lands on the southern slopes of Neasden hill were used not only for hay and other crops but also, in the mid-19th century, the Willesden paddocks were famous horse-training grounds. In 1825, one of the Finch family built Dollis Hill House on the southern side of 'Bower Lane' with Dollis Hill farm still on the north side. Some fifty years later it was taken over by Lord Aberdeen, a great friend of the Liberal statesman, William Gladstone. The Prime Minister used to stay at the house in the 1880s to get away from the pressures of Parliament and the bustle of town. He would go to church at St Andrews, Neasden-cum-Kingsbury. Did he walk down to the Welsh Harp and across the dam-top (certainly not allowed today)? George Eliot's novel *Daniel Deronda* has a scene set in the drawing room of the house.

A Mr. H. K. North writing in the local paper in 1926 of the Willesden of 50 years earlier, recalled:

We had to walk from White Hart-lane to Portsdown terrace, Kilburn, for pills or salt. To Paddington we had to tramp for provisions and drapery. We did our shopping, turned homewards, and got into Willesden-lane; it was a common occurrence to slip into the ditch up to your knees in water ... Our milk we got from a milkman; he had a pair of yokes on his shoulders and two milk cans ... Our water came from Mr Kilby's well at Queenstown... we could go to the pump and get it ourselves at 1/2d per pail, or we could go to Dickeringson farm near Villiers-road, one hour in the morning and one at night, free.

The Round House stood opposite the *White Hart* and when a prisoner was taken he was in the lock-up until morning and then taken to Marylebone Police Court.

Despite the extensive expansion of the Victorian suburb, large tracts of Willesden remained virtually untouched by the hand of the developer and builder.

Foley takes us, as already mentioned, along those beloved byways:

A good view of Brent Reservoir (or Hendon Lake) opens upon us—the cattle grazing on the grassy slopes of Dollis Hill [which sloped down north-wards to the water, no North Circular Road to impede the walk] or wading knee deep in one of the reedy inlets on that southern shore; the different lines of elms and hedgerows that curve gently to the water's edge on the opposite side or form little

52. The Round House near the *Six Bells* was used as a constable's lock-up.

promontories along the margin. The boats dotted about, with here and there a tiny white sail standing out against the blue water with the wooded knoll of Wembley crowning the furthest point over a mile away.

(That is the picture which has hardly changed in nearly a hundred years as seen from near the former Welsh Harp station.)

Such were Sherrick Green on the Slade Brook, Neasden ('a few scattered cottages, a fair sprinkling of good old houses planted in large grounds') and Dollis Hill.

Another memoir of Willesden was published in 1954 in the *Willesden Chronicle*, taken from an article in the *Middlesex Quarterly* by B. C Dexter, a Willesden council architect and a local historian. He was writing of the district in the 1890s.

Up to the 1890's it was possible to ... cross the fields from the Harrow road to Willesden (as described by Harrison Ainsworth in "Jack Sheppard") ... pass a pond much favoured by the local youth for fishing newts and crossing the summit of a hill [ie Mount Pleasant] one overlooked Willesden.

At Harlesden there was a considerable extent of open land and it was possible to stand on the Harrow Road bridges over the L & NW Railway and have a view scarcely broken by a building, and the walk across the fields from Acton Lane to Stonebridge was a

pleasant country ramble ... The patches of vacant land in the southern part of Kilburn were an attraction to strolling showmen in the 1880 period. Not only were there the usual collection of roundabouts and swings but cheapjacks set up their vans and did a good trade...

The Willesden Board 1875-1895

The achievements of the Willesden Board in its 20 years' existence were substantial. After a hesitant start due to unfamiliarity with the tasks imposed on, and then accepted by, the new members, they began to use their responsible position for the benefit of the expanding township.

Drainage was uppermost in the minds of the Board members. Oscar Claude Robson, the dedicated Surveyor to the Board, compiled a substantial assessment of the very situation which had contributed to the formation of the Local Board. He found that Kilburn was, by now, well sewered by egg-shaped outfall sewers flowing into the Ranelagh sewer of the Metropolitan network. The Mapesbury district (between Kilburn and the Shoot-up-Hill ridge) had some drains along its main roads which sufficed for the present. Harlesden, although its outlying areas would present problems, had been partially drained in 1870. Kensal Green had no regular system of sewers—privies and water closets drained into old broken-down pipes. However, it was rural

Willesden, the northern half of which drained into
the Brent itself, which was in the worst situation.

Robson wrote in his 1876 report:

The houses are in most cases provided with
water closets which, together with all household refuse water, drain into cesspools, the
overflow from which either directly drains into
open ditches or watercourses or into old brick
or pipe sewers emptying into such watercourses. These during the summer, being but
scantily supplied with rainwater, become sluggish in flow or stagnate entirely and assume
the character of elongated open cess-pools giving off fetid and noxious odours in close con-
tiguity to houses and main roads ...

The sewage often entered the ditch in the
same condition as it left the house.

Seldom has there been a more graphic public
report. He went on to urge that earth closets should
be replaced by a system connected to mains
drainage. However, the Board, conscious of its
new position but equally aware of the ratepayers'
wrath, deferred a decision. Several more reports
were produced; ratepayers' protests forced a public
enquiry and it was not until October 1885 that the
scheme was sanctioned. A sewerage network was
built which formed the basis of today's underground drainage system and enabled Willesden to
develop speedily.

By 1875 there were some 25 miles of road in
Willesden. Mostly the surface was gravel, crushed
by roller; some was macadamised. Robson brought
about a gradual but inexorable transition towards
good roads. In 1886 he was overjoyed to be given
permission to buy a steamroller—a matter of such
significance that it was remembered nine years later
in the retrospective survey of Willesden 1875-94
in the local paper.

The Local Board also set about the task of
improving the lighting of the streets. It recognised
that the safety of its citizens at night depended
partly on an efficient police force but also on
well-lit roads. Gas lighting was started in 1813 by
the Gas Light and Coke Company at Westminster.
It reached Willesden areas in the 1860s. By the
time the Board was elected there were 248 street
lamps. It was essential that, as roads were extended
and new ones built, gas lighting be provided.
Another of Robson's invaluable reports reveals
that in 1883 there were 27 new lamps needed in
Edgware Road, Willesden Lane and so on, at a
cost of £113 10s. 6d.

At the end of 1875, the excellent Dr. George
Danfort Thomas, Medical Officer of Health,
presented his first annual report, covering nuisance
abatement and health inspections. His reports paint

53. Waterloo Farm, the site of Willesden's Town
Hall.

a picture of overcrowding and the resulting disease
and fatalities. He was not above reminding the
Board that a healthy body leads to a healthy mind
and called for the setting up of public libraries and
better school attendance.

Dr. Thomas showed there were 1,746 houses
with 13,968 inhabitants in the 'Urban portion', of
Willesden, that is Kilburn, with its sewage draining
into main sewers. The rest of the area, the 'Rural
portion', had only 605 houses with a population of
4,175, draining into open ditches or open privies.

He was able to say that only 250 of the parish's
4,382 acres were built on—the rest, apart from
the Paddington and the Jewish cemeteries, being
meadow or agricultural land.

By 1894, at the end of the Board's period of
service, Dr. Skinner, by then MOH, was reporting
on improvements in general health over the
previous year. The total population was estimated
at 73,640, with Kilburn still populous and overcrowded with 11 persons on average to each house
compared with six in the rest of the parish. These
annual reports will fascinate anyone who wishes
to study the realities of local life of the period.

The most important legacy of the Local Board
was the quintessentially Victorian Board Offices,
later to become those of the district council and,
eventually, Willesden's town hall. The building
was the subject of a competition won by Newman
and Newman. The plans were laid at the end of the
1880s and it was built on the site of Waterloo
Farm, in Dyne Road, Kilburn. It was opened by
James Stewart, the chairman of the Local Board,
in November 1891. Its council chamber must have
been comfortable for 15 members, barely worse
for the 21 who formed the first district council, but

54. Willesden hospital, *c*.1910.

less easy for the 52 members of the mature borough council. For all its charm and despite the local history bound up in it, there was not deemed to be enough architectural merit to save it when Willesden became part of Brent. It was pulled down to make way for much needed housing, bearing the name James Stewart House.

Some of the other public buildings of the period should be mentioned. The benefactions of John Passmore Edwards, a Cornishman, extended to public libraries and hospitals. In 1892, the Willesden Cottage Hospital was built thanks to his philanthropy. It was also designed by Newman and Newman and was opened by Mr. A. J. Balfour (a leading Conservative politician and a future prime minister) and his daughter. A municipal hospital for infectious diseases was initiated by the Local Board at Neasden in 1894 on the site of the old marsh. It was demolished in the late 1980s to make way for housing.

The grounds contain the Slade Brook—on the south side of the hospital is the school (now closed) which took its name from the almost hidden stream (a suggestion put forward by the author).

Chapter 11

Moving On

Watkin and the Metropolitan Railway

Edward William Watkin (1819-1901) was born in Manchester. He worked for the L.N.W.R. under Mark Huish, went to the Manchester, Sheffield and Lincolnshire (MSL), became chairman, then an M.P., knighted in 1868 and made a baronet in 1880. One of his visions was a railway from Manchester to Paris so that he added to his first chairmanship those of the South Eastern Railway, the Metropolitan Railway and the Channel Tunnel Company. Yet much of what he touched turned to dross.

The Metropolitan Railway opened the first underground line in 1863. In 1879, the Metropolitan extension at last broke out of the tunnel at Swiss Cottage, made for West Hampstead and then, by a massive bridge over the Edgware Road at Kilburn (which was not replaced until almost exactly one hundred years later), leapt into Willesden. Its first stations in the district were at Kilburn and Brondesbury and at Willesden Green, opened on 24 November 1879. The Kingsbury and Harrow Joint Committee was in being, all ready to extend the line to Harrow-on-the-Hill.

An intermediate station was built to serve the two small villages after which it was named, Kingsbury and Neasden. To bring traffic to the station, the Metropolitan Company arranged with a local livery stable for a 22-seater two-horse bus to make six round trips from Harlesden each week day at a fare of 2d.—this ran from 1880 to 1885.

The permanent way included some special technical features and the architecture, particularly of Harrow station, was praised. The opening of the line was heralded by festivities at the *King's Head*, Harrow, with free trips to Willesden Green. The Metropolitan line was extended, in stages, outwards, reaching Aylesbury in 1892. It was not always the success it claimed to provide. W. S. Gilbert wrote to the directors of the company: 'Saturday mornings, though occurring at frequent and well-regulated intervals, always seem to take this railway by surprise.'

The effect of the new railway, with its squat steam trains and green (later brown) livery, initially operating 36 trains a day in each direction (apart from a 'church interval' on Sunday) was to open up the heart of Willesden to development.

The extension to Harrow involved crossing the northern half of Wembley Park which was sold to the Company by the Rev. J. G. Gray; he then decided to sell the rest of the Park but died before the purchase was completed. The Railway Company visualised a great amusement ground which would attract visitors from all over London, conveyed thither by their trains. The crowning glory, as Watkin himself planned, was to be a tower to rival the newly-built Eiffel Tower. Although the site is in Wembley, for a short while it dominated

55. Sir Edward Watkin, the railway king.

56.   The Metropolitan Railway—Kingsbury and Neasden station, *c*.1910, opening up the suburbs with electric trains.

the landscape over the river Brent plain at Stonebridge—just as the stadium does today.

It turned out to be Watkin's Folly. By September 1895, the first platform 155 ft. above the ground was completed and in May the following year, with lifts installed, it was opened to the public.

The Metropolitan Company built a station at Wembley Park, opened in May 1894, to serve the new amusement park and Tower. For all this variety, Wembley Park was not a success, the Tower being the first to fail, being closed to the public in 1902 and demolished by explosives in 1907.

Watkin had been pressing on with his last great scheme, the linking of the MSL with London. This was to become, in 1889, the Great Central Railway. Though never a great success, since the other mainline railways had creamed the rich traffic, it survived. The earlier intention was to link with the Metropolitan at Aylesbury, run on to Baker Street and then through London to link with the South East and Chatham. If the Channel tunnel had been built, the dream of Manchester to Paris by train would have been realised—the Great Central was an essential link.

Unfortunately, the Metropolitan, despite Watkin's connections, were difficult allies and the

Great Central had to decide on its own terminus at Marylebone. The 'Met' provided widened lines— quadrupling of the track from Harrow to Canfield Place whence the G.C.R.'s own lines ran into Marylebone (opened in 1898). There were junctions at Neasden (called Brent North and South) with the Midland line which ran through Gladstone Park to Acton, but no stations were allowed to be built on this stretch of the line and thus no direct benefit to Willesden from the new trunk route.

A development resulting from both the Metropolitan and the Great Central lines passing through Willesden was workers' housing. The older railway established a big engineering works at Neasden in the early 1880's—in the heart of green fields where the nearest industry was Jackman's smithy. Homes for the work force were provided in a compact estate near Kingsbury bridge. (Sir Edward Watkin, while admitting it might cost the company one per cent, said—wisely and in advance of his time—'my experience is that we gain indirectly a great benefit by practically improving the comfort of the people whom we employ'.)

The street names reflected the Metropolitan Railway's interests: originally Quainton and Verney, and later Aylesbury (1904) and Chesham (1920s) Streets—all names of termini or junctions out in Buckinghamshire. A small church,

57. Neasden railway works. A staff outing in 1937.

58. Quainton Street was built in the 1880s. It is shown here in 1961 before the power station was demolished.

St Saviour's, was built by E. J. Tarver at the corner of Quainton Street and Neasden Lane—the brick gate pillars are still there (1994). It is a quiet backwater with additional houses built by Willesden council in the 1920s and two schools erected in the 1970s. (One primary, one secondary, which was closed in 1989.)

Towards the end of the century, the Great Central Railway—the last of the main line railways to run into the Metropolis—built a staff colony to house workshopmen and locomotive drivers from the Neasden Depot. This was at Gresham and Woodheyes Roads where there was also built a church for the family estate. The roads led into Dog Lane—the North Circular Road had not yet arrived to massacre the old road layout.

Omnibuses and the 'New' Trams
In 1870 an omnibus was advertised in the *Kilburn Times* running from Praed Street to the Spotted Dog Pleasure Gardens at Willesden Green, leaving Praed Street at half past 1 o'clock every Sunday—fare 1s. 6d. (which was fairly expensive). Other more frequent horse-drawn services ran from the *Lord Palmerston* on the Edgware Road to Town. The Fenchurch Street bus was dark green, ran every 6 or 7 minutes and the fare all the way was 6d. On

Sunday the service was extended to Whitechapel.

To Charing Cross ran a light red bus with a broad white band. A dark red bus went to Victoria for 5d., stopping at the *Cock* (eventually this became the 16 bus route). Passengers who were fortunate enough to join at the start of the journey found seats, hard and unsprung, inside; the later arrivals clambered on the roof. Mr. Gladstone averred that the best way to see London was from the top of an omnibus.

By 1895 a large network of horse buses operated to the south of Willesden. From the *Falcon* at Queen's Park a red bus went to Victoria, another to Charing Cross and a yellow one to London Bridge (in part antecedents of the 36 and 6 of later and present days), while an alternative 'yellow' route terminated at the *William IV* at Kensal Green. A 'local' service, a green fourpenny bus, ran from Harlesden via Willesden Lane to Kilburn. Others served different combinations of starting points in Willesden, finishing in or near the City.

On the Kilburn to Liverpool Street route there was a big, broad-shouldered, cleanshaven, swarthy driver with a perpetual smile and a 'hail fellow well met' air, whose technique would have stood him in good stead as a Roman charioteer. As the bus was full up at the start, he would stop for no-

59.   Horse-bus terminus at Cricklewood in the early 1900s. Note the advertisement for the renowned young pianist, Mark Hambourg.

60.   Kilburn High Road, 1886.

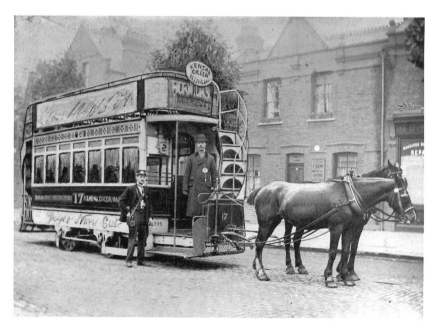

61.   The last workman's horse-tram along the Harrow Road, *c.*1905.

one, his vehicle darted in, out and round the rest of the traffic. He was known as 'Darkey' and was said to have a special guardian angel.

The first tramway—horse-drawn—of course, in North West London was the two-and-a-half mile stretch from Amberley Road along the Harrow Road to Harlesden Green (with a branch, short lived, to Carlton Vale). It was opened in 1888 with a depot at Trenmar Gardens, College Park (just outside the Willesden boundary). Twopence was the fare all the way and the passengers could sit inside the red and brown carriages, out of the weather, or climb the curved stairway to the upper deck. For a 13-hour day the drivers of the fleet of 20 cars were paid 5s. 9d.—standing in an open cab, with moustaches freezing in the winter!

Pubs Through the Ages
Thomas Clutterbuck and his family had extensive interests as brewers and licensees in many villages in north-west Middlesex. They built or rebuilt many inns in the late 18th and early 19th centuries.

An inn-token (in common use when change was short) exists for the *Anchor and Cable* in Harlesden bearing those emblems and dated at Willesden, 1670. The *Old Crown* is now on the same site on what used to be called Harlesden

Green (there are over one thousand inns called *Crown* in England). The *Green Man* and the *Royal Oak* stand at the eastern end of the Green, with the *Elmtree* opposite both of them, which seems to be of 19th-century origin.

The *Coach and Horses* at Stonebridge was yet another inn which served the traveller as well as the villager. It lay near the oxbow of the Brent where the old stone bridge had, for hundreds of years, allowed a dry passage over the river. It was also a resort for anglers even up to one hundred years ago. It had associations with the artist, George Morland (1762/3-1804), a fine painter with many Brent connections who lived his sad life in and out of public houses, many of which he used in his paintings. These include the *Plough* on the Hammersmith side of Harrow Road at Kensal Green and the *Red Lion* and the *Bell* at Kilburn. *At the Door of the Red Lion* hangs in the Tate Gallery and *Le Halte* in the Louvre (Paris) bears the inn sign of the *Bell*. Morland drank excessively and his marriage was soon in trouble. He once offered to repaint the inn sign at the *Coach and Horses* but lost it and could not face the innkeeper's wife, Mrs. Read, again! In the 1890s, the pub was being run by 'Jumbo Eccleston', who weighed 40 stone and had to have a special pony

62. *Coach and Horses*, Stonebridge, *c*.1900.

and trap in which to travel around. He built Eccleston Place and Mews in Wembley. He also ran the *Canterbury Arms* in South Kilburn.

Elsewhere in Willesden parish, as befits its age and size, there were inns like the *Spotted Dog* on Willesden Green, described in 1792 as 'being a well accostomed Publick House'. It became a favourite place of resort for mid-Victorian Londoners who would drive out 'to the country'. It was also, for a time, the starting point of horse-buses to Town. The Willesden Local Board held its first public dinner here. The *Six Bells* established in 1708 was, for many years, the meeting place for St Mary's vestry. It was demolished in 1961 but has lasting fame in the pages of Harrison Ainsworth's *Jack Sheppard*. Almost opposite was the *White Hart* and nearby the *White Horse* which was, for a time in the mid-19th century, used also as a post office.

The coming of the canal encouraged trippers, as well as the canal workers, to seek refreshment. Thus there is a pertinently named *Pleasure Boat Inn* where the Ealing Road crosses the canal and, further east, the *Junction Arms* at Lower Place or

East Twyford as it was known at the time of the construction of the canal.

The development of Kilburn in the latter half of the 19th century was accompanied by the building of many new public houses, just one of the many indications of a growing township. In quick succession came the *Prince of Wales, Duke of Cambridge, Canterbury Arms, Brondesbury Arms, Sir Robert Peel* and the *Falcon*, bearing names with obvious mid-Victorian appeal or local connections. Kensal was almost as well served. In addition to the *Plough* at the corner of Ladbroke Grove, there was the *Grey Horse* and the *Old Plough* in, or near, Kilburn Lane. Along Harrow Road was the *King William IV* and all these benefited from Kensal Green cemetery which brought, at first, building workers and then cemetery workers, leading to a larger Kensal Green village.

As Willesden grew, so did the number of public houses (except in the area in which ran the writ of the Ecclesiastical Commissioners).

Along Kilburn High Road came the *Rifle Volunteer* and the *Victoria* at the corner of Willesden Lane (both under different names to-

63. The *Spotted Dog*, Willesden Green, 1879, is shown advertising the opening of the Metropolitan extension to Harrow.

day reflecting the Irish community). The *North London*, obviously near Brondesbury station, was where the Willesden Local Board met before it obtained Hampton House. Another unsurprising name was the *Windmill* in Cricklewood, while further north, serving the developments in the late 19th century, was the aptly named *Cricklewood Hotel*. On the opposite side of the road, the *Crown* was both a hostelry and a location for bus and tram terminals.

Near the crossing, by the Edgware Road, of the river Brent, where it enters the reservoir, on the very boundary of Willesden, was the *Old Welsh Harp*, known to the Victorians by repute and by song as 'the jolliest place that's out'. From about 1859, when it was rebuilt, to 1889, it was run and popularised by William Perkins Warner, a Crimean War veteran and the son of the owner of Blackbird Farm at Neasden.

After the First World War many new estates were built and with them came, as might be expected, the new public houses. The *Ox and Gate* is one of the few new public houses in East Willesden basing its punning name on the old prebendal Oxgate Estate.

The North Circular Road has its inns to cater for the thirsty traveller. The *Abbey* is very much a roadside inn, also available to local industry since there is little housing nearby, as is the case with the *Plumes* on the Park Royal Estate. The *Pantiles*, a name reflecting its architecture and its period, serves not only thirsty travellers using the arterial road but also the housing estate of St Raphael's, now much enlarged since the inn was first built.

The 1980s saw a boom in new drinking establishments following the relaxing of licensing laws—in Neasden, along Willesden High Road and elsewhere.

Background To Living

'A nation of shopkeepers' (a phrase from Adam Smith quoted disparagingly by Napoleon) is never so well borne out as in our study of the burgeoning township of Willesden. In 1885 plans were submitted for 17 shops in Willesden; in 1886 there were 108 plans deposited. Shops spread gradually along the Kilburn High Road. Street hawkers survived well after the Second World War, along the High Road. The buildings were in a series of 'terraces', solidly built structures with shops on the ground floor and two or three storeys of housing above. James Stewart, one of the founders of the district, had a draper's shop in Manor Terrace between Oxford and Cambridge Roads.

Similar examples on both sides of the road up to Kilburn station were built gradually in a series of developments up to the end of the century.

Many of the shopping premises of Victorian Kilburn remain—indeed the Kilburn Square development is the only really modern creation. Some were houses with the present shops built on the former front gardens—this would seem to be true of the shops between Brondesbury Road and Brondesbury Villas. (Another shopping street where the glass-fronts conceal quite attractive houses behind is Craven Park Road. It is worth a stretch of the neck to see the triangular pediments, semi-circular window arches, the proportions of

64. Kilburn Square in 1961, before redevelopment.

65. Kilburn High Road, c.1895 showing James Crook, funeral furnishers, and a delivery boy and bicycle.

66. Kilburn High Road, c.1904 with B. B. Evans' shop, which was used by everyone in Willesden and Hampstead. At one time Mr. Evans was a Willesden councillor.

the windows on the several storeys and the roof-line.) In Kilburn High Road, one particularly attractive building is the house and premises of James Crook, funeral undertaker, at the corner with Buckley Road—the firm have been in existence in Kilburn since the early 19th century.

B. B. (Benjamin Beardmore) Evans was a lively Welshman who came to London to make his fortune. He opened a small shop in 1897, in the Kilburn High Road (on the Hampstead side of the road). It became the biggest in north-west London despite two disastrous fires from each of which it recovered. Evans was a Willesden coun-cillor for a term; he died in 1915 but the firm survived until 1971.

Willesden Green shopping centre, stretching virtually unbroken from the High Road at Chapel End to Willesden Green station, contained one of the only two department stores in Brent—both run by the London Co-operative Society (the Co-op)—the other being at Burnt Oak. (A third shop was in Kilburn High Road, though on the Hampstead side, near the station.) The street, at its western end, is mainly late Victorian—the police station is dated 1896—while the Walm Lane end is mainly post-First World War. Efforts to brighten the façades and improve the ambience were envisaged under the 1980s Willesden District Plan.

Between 1908-1910, new shopping centres were established at Kensal Rise, Salusbury Road, and Stonebridge as well as substantial increases at Cricklewood Broadway. As new housing sprang up further away from these centres, small groups of shops were developed to serve local needs. Examples are in Chapter Road and Okehampton Road and, later on (from 1920) Village Way, Sidmouth Parade and College Road (Kensal Rise).

A major shopping centre developed at Neasden. It was built to serve the large new post-First World War estates. Neasden was then the most up-to-date shopping centre within Willesden but, sited on the junction of two main traffic arteries, its location made it dangerous for shoppers.

The corner shop which finds its place in the older areas—like the ones in Hamilton Road serving Dollis Hill—was not so often found in these rather grand estates.

Banks have some delusions of grandeur. Such, for example, are the Bank Chambers at the corner of Chichele Road and Cricklewood Broadway or Barclays Bank at the eastern end of Willesden Green High Road—survivors in their original construction.

In Harlesden, served by a horse-bus to London, a well-organised community had come into existence, All Souls' church at one end and inns at the other. An 1875 directory reveals four inns (*the Crown, Green Man, Royal Oak* and the *Elm Tree*—the *Willesden Junction Hotel* was opened a few years later), a coal agent, a saddler- and harness-maker, sweets dealer, at least three butchers, Sam Spatchett, smith, confectioner, several boot- and

67. The Co-op Store, High Road, Willesden Green, now demolished and replaced by housing.

68. Mr. Dickens of Carter Paterson in Hawthorn Road, *c*.1900.

69. H. Gibbs, grocer, Grange Road, *c*.1900.

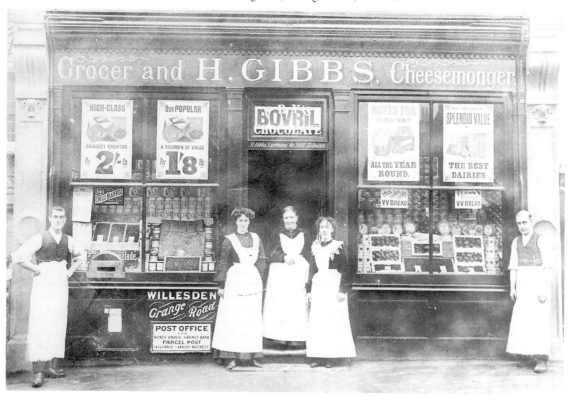

70.   A corner shop at 39 Keslake Road.

71.   Harlesden Manor Farm, which later became Beesons works.

shoe-makers a post office combined with draper, a dressmaker, corndealer, florist (an early version of the Penn Craft shop), several grocers, fishmongers, a coffee room, a brush and glass warehouse, a number of farriers of course, a 'berlin wool' warehouse, a baker or two, another draper, a carpenter, a wheelwright and a tailor. This is not a bad list for any 'core' of shopping today, give or take a few trades that have lapsed or risen in the past century. The population of Harlesden was about two thousand and growing fast.

This part of Willesden was lush farmland until, in a few short years, the rush for urbanisation obliterated Sellon's Farm, the Manor Farm, Bramshill Lodge and the Grange. Only Roundwood House and Farm were (temporarily) saved—now the park of the same name.

By 1910, there were local firms which survived for many years—Karl Schworrer the jeweller, Penn Craft the florist, Strange and Chitham, outfitters, Claude Bastable, builder, Hedley Molyneux, stationers, Beeson Bros., hardware, Horace Borer, outfitter. A full range of shops was now available—indeed by the beginning of the century the shape of Harlesden was set and it has hardly changed since—which is, perhaps, its biggest problem. Only the section from the library to Craven Park remained mainly residential until the 1930s and then development, particularly on the west side, overwhelmed most of the houses—the Odeon, in particular, revitalising, for a time, the ageing shopping street. The cinema has itself has been replaced by a handsome block of housing association flats.

Harlesden shopping centre is a good example to illustrate the growth of a Brent village. It has an elongated Z-shape, stretching from near the *Royal Oak*, past the Jubilee Clock, right through to Craven Park where a firm of estate agents (at one time, Deason and Lester) in a century-old building continues to operate on an island site created for traffic purposes. Although the buildings are mostly late Victorian, the High Street retains something of the characteristics of the old village green.

Chapter 12

Big Houses, Big Names in Victorian Willesden

Big Houses

The manor house, standing in its own parkland, was the visual symbol of the country gentleman of Victorian times. It is a sad comment on 'progress' that so few of them remain in urban areas like ours. Brondesbury House was described as having no regularity of architectural character but was fairly commodious and surrounded by extensive and well-arranged grounds, designed by Humphry Repton, one of the most famous of British landscapers.

Heathfield Lodge lent its name to the present Heathfield Park but Pheasantfield became Blenheim Gardens and its name was lost, as was that of Brierley Villa, the home at one time of F. A. Wood.

Roundwood House dates from the early 19th century, the land belonging to James Denew, to C. R. Ayres and in 1838 to Lord Decies. His son-in-law Lord Ernest (Brudenell) Bruce occupied it

in the 1850s; he was also related to Lord Cardigan (of Charge of the Light Brigade fame) and to the Craven family from whom nearby Craven Park derives its name. George Furness (*see below*) was, in 1856, wealthy enough to buy the house from Lord Decies. He and his family (which included George J Furness, Willesden West M.P. 1922/23) occupied it until 1935. The house was sold to Willesden council in 1937, when a sale of effects meant that some Willesden citizens obtained memorials of Roundwood House and the Furness family. It was later pulled down, the grounds added to Roundwood Park and the site used for an old people's home and a youth centre.

Mapesbury House, which was probably an estate building dating way back to Tudor times (traces of the old manorial building and a moat were found when it was demolished), was rebuilt in the early 19th century. It was then an attractive residence with a large pediment above the first

72. Roundwood House, *c.*1895. It is possibly the Furness family at play on the lawn.

73. *(Above left)* Mapesbury House, *c.*1905.

74. *(Above right)* Neasden House, *c.*1900. The house has had many uses having been at times manor house, golf clubhouse and flats.

floor, but in 1925 it succumbed to the post-First World War pressure for development, replaced by Deerhurst and Coverdale Roads.

Neasden House on top of the hill came into the possession of John Nicoll and later of J. W. Prout. On the other side of the road that led from Willesden to Kingsbury was The Grove, built by Dr. Thomas Wingfield in the early 1700s; later it was owned by Lord George Carpenter M.P. and then acquired by James Hall in the early 1800s. One of the buildings associated with The Grove was the house now known as The Grange, home of the local history museum. Squire Hall had kennels for his

hunting dogs at the back of the house and the Neasden Harrier Pack became famous. There were dogs also at Neasden House. The packs were dispersed in mid-century but the name lingers on in Dog Lane. According to Potter there was a Dog Kennel Wood just south of Lansdowne Grove. Henry Finch owned Dollis Hill House and William P. Warner owned Oxgate in Dog Kennel Lane, Dollis Hill.

In 1806 at West Twyford, Thomas Willan, a stage-coach proprietor, bought the small farm house and filled in the moat. He had W. Atkinson—who later erected Abbotsford for Sir Walter Scott—

75. The Grove was built in the early 18th century and was home to the Prout family. This photograph dates from 1920. The house was demolished in 1937.

76. *(Above left)* Neasden Harriers in the 1840s; the harrriers formed part of Willesden's famous horse-racing activity.

77. *(Above right)* The Grange, pictured here from Neasden Green. A watercolour by C. E. Donner.

build a large mansion with 'Cockney-Gothic' battlemented towers, calling it grandly Twyford Abbey—although there was no religious connection. Yet, prophetically, it did obtain such a link when, in 1902, it was bought by the Alexian Fathers (a Catholic Order) as a rest home. It is the one big house mentioned here, other than the Grange, which is still standing.

Personalities in Victorian Willesden

William Harrison Ainsworth (1805-1882) came from a Lancashire family and adopted his mother's maiden name as well as his father's surname. He was born and educated in Manchester. On the death of his father in 1824, he went to London to complete his legal training. A handsome young man, he married Fanny Ebers, who lived at the Elms in Kilburn, in 1826. She bore him three daughters. He had dabbled in literary pieces before and, while studying law, *Rookwood* (which includes Dick Turpin's ride to York) was written at the Elms and published in 1834 (its description of Kilburn is fictitious, setting a scene at the *Jack Falstaff*, i.e. the *Cock Inn*).

The next year, having separated from his wife, he moved to Kensal Lodge. Charles Dickens and John Forster were among the frequent guests; so was Thackeray, another lawyer manqué. A stream of books poured forth, nearly one a year, from then almost until his death.

In 1841, Ainsworth moved next door to Kensal Manor House. He became a churchwarden at St Mary's church and in 1850 a member of the restoration committee under the Rev. Knapp.

He made much use of his love of the local scene in such novels as *Old St. Paul's* and especially in *Jack Sheppard* where he fictitiously locates a number of the highwayman's exploits in the area. The descriptions of Neasden, Dollis Hill and Willesden give a clear and vivid picture of the countryside around his home—so much so that it became known as 'The Jack Sheppard County'—and there may still be people convinced by Ainsworth's writing that the highwayman was buried in Willesden churchyard.

However, his fame and his circle of friends declined. Late in life he married again—Sarah Wells, who, in 1867, bore him yet another daughter. He died in January 1882 and is buried in Kensal Green cemetery.

78. The novelist Harrison Ainsworth aged 34.

George Furness (1820-1906), the father of modern Willesden, was born in Longstone, Derbyshire (hence Longstone Avenue). As a young man he seized an opportunity to take part in railway contracting at an early stage in the expansion of that form of transport, in the Midlands near his home in 1842 and then in France.

Gradually he built up a large business and became famous in the civil engineering world. He obtained the largest of the contracts in connection with the main drainage of London, worth two-thirds of a million pounds. He built, with the backing of the engineer Bazalgette, a considerable portion of the Thames Embankment from Westminster Bridge to Somerset House (although his was not the lowest tender). He constructed the railway in Pernambuco, Brazil and for 30 years carried out dredging contracts in Italy (recalled in road names: Spezia, Palermo, Leghorn and Ancona Roads). His greatest contract abroad was the one awarded, magnanimously, by the Russian government for the restoration of public works in Odessa damaged in the Crimean War 1854-56 (thus Odessa Road). He was considered by his contemporaries as a reliable contractor, to rank with Brassey and John Aird.

Locally, he built in Cricklewood, Harlesden (Furness Road was named for, not by, him) and elsewhere in Willesden. More important than this was his contribution to local government. Although opposed to the formation of the Local Board, he became its first Chairman; he was also one of the first representatives on the Middlesex County Council, sat on the Hendon Board of Guardians and the Willesden School Board. In public office his tenacity of purpose, liberal views and ready regard for divergent opinion were as noticeable as in his private and professional life. He was an Evangelical churchman and, in the old days when the parish Vestry was of real importance and meant hard fighting, for many years he secured triumphant election as the people's Churchwarden. He was a tall man described as a 'dear old country squire'. He owned Roundwood House and the Willesden Brick Works at Chambers Lane and was regarded as a generous and genial master. He married an Italian girl and had two sons (one of whom became M.P. for West Willesden) and two daughters. He was a self-made man who conquered many obstacles and was left unspoilt by the wealth he attained.

Chapter 13

Dedicated to God

The Early Willesden Churches

Willesden's parish church of St Mary's, before the Reformation, was a well-known centre for pilgrimage (particularly the 'Black Virgin of Willesden'). Brasses in the church of long-deceased residents present us with a miniature history book of the parish: Bartholemew of Willesden; Dr. William Lichfield, vicar in the early 16th century (wearing a fur hat and long scarf—most suitable for a chilly church in a damp wood near the marshy river); and several of the Roberts family.

For hundreds of years, the church was also the focus of local secular activities. The vestry was responsible for law and order, poor relief, ale-conning (assessing the strength of beer) and so on. The absence of a dominant family or squire (apart from Sir William Roberts in the 17th century) gave more strength to the vestry. By the beginning of the 19th century, St Mary's was again dilapidated, but two stages of restoration in the middle and latter parts of the century, and again in the 1930s, have preserved its structure.

In 1825 a proprietary chapel was erected in Kilburn (near the *Cock Inn*) to serve the village, part of which was in Hampstead. It was known as the chapel in the country. Ten years later, it was rebuilt as St Paul's church, Kilburn Square, the only church on the main road between Marble Arch and Edgware, a plain building without tower or chancel but comfortable inside. In 1867 the congregation split when Holy Trinity was opened a short distance away in Brondesbury Road. It went through a lean period from which it was saved by the Rev. Bonavia-Hunt (later head of Kilburn Grammar School). He was an accomplished musician as well as a keen educationalist and made St Paul's a church music centre, but he was unable to obtain consecration for it until 1897. By 1925 the building was in need of immediate repair to secure it against very serious dilapidation but funds were not forthcoming. It closed in May 1935 and was pulled down.

Dr. C. W. Williams, Principal of the North London Collegiate Boys' School at Camden Town knew Brondesbury well. In 1864, he saw the probability of expansion of the area and encouraged the small but well-to-do community of Brondesbury which made the first real 'challenge' to St Mary's; Christ Church was built in 1866 and the new parish created. Designed by C. R. B. King, the tower and its spire were a prominent feature on the hill slope. It was consecrated on 21 November 1866. In 1889, Dr. Williams' son succeeded him and gradually the church began to prosper. During the Second World War a land mine severely damaged the church, but it was later restored. In 1990 much of the church was imaginatively converted into flats.

79. St Paul's, Kilburn Square, *c*.1890, shown 'To Let'.

80. Christ Church,
Brondesbury, *c*.1900.

Meanwhile in Harlesden the growing population of that expanding village created a demand for a local church. Services were started as early as 1858 and nine years later, in 1867, a temporary iron-built structure was erected. Then, to serve the new parish created in 1875, an exciting new church, All Souls', designed by E. J. Tarver as an octagon, was opened in 1879 by the Bishop of London.

The architects, F. and F. J. Francis, were responsible for the now-vanished Holy Trinity in Kilburn, 1867 and for St John's, 1871, at the corner of Rudolph Road and Princess Road, the first in South Kilburn. This is over-awed by its neighbour, the magnificent masterpiece of J. L. Pearson, St Augustine's, consecrated in 1880. Geographically located in Paddington (but with much of the parish lying in Willesden), its spire, completed 18 years after the main church building, rises 254 ft., and still dominates the Kilburn scene, despite the high-rise flats.

In Willesden Green High Road, St Andrew's, designed by James Brooks, was consecrated in 1887. Its large brick-built Early English style is one of the few buildings of distinction in the High Road (perhaps the only other one is the entrance to the Central library—at one time threatened with destruction by council 'improvers'). Pevsner describes it as 'stately if somewhat dull' but adds that it provides a typical contrast to the old village church—St Mary's.

The expansion of Stonebridge created a need which was met by the imposing bulk of St Michael's and All Angels in 1891. It still stands, somewhat overshadowed by new tower blocks which have replaced the 16 Victorian streets for whose residents it was built.

In Cricklewood, the people of the larger houses on Walm Lane and the town houses round the eastern end of Anson Road called for a religious meeting place. A small hall was erected, preceding the building of the main church. This original building was later taken over by the council and renamed Anson Hall. St Gabriel's church itself was consecrated in 1897 by Bishop Creighton. Three years later, on 27 July 1900, it was struck by lightning and the roof of the nave destroyed.

When Mortimer Road was built, a space for a church was left in the land given by All Souls' College. As far back as 1883, the curate of St John's, Kensal Green, started mission work in a potato shop in the Harrow Road, calling it the Christ Church Mission, College Park. A proposal for a memorial to Dean Vaughan (Headmaster of Harrow 1844-59) was fulfilled when, in July 1899, Princess Henry of Battenberg laid the foundation stone in Mortimer Road. A year later the church, designed by J. E. K. and J. P. Cutts (known for 'muscular' brick churches—they also designed St Lawrence and St Anne's) was dedicated by the Bishop of London and the name changed from Christ Church to St Martin (after a link between Vaughan and a church of the same name in Leicester).

At one time it was proposed that St Matthew's church should be a memorial to Charles Reade, the

81.   St Gabriel's church. It was struck by lightning in 1900.

novelist (author of *The Cloister and the Hearth*, buried in Willesden churchyard; for some time the district was referred to officially by his name). St Matthew was the name adopted for a mission church built in the fields at the bottom of St Mary's Road to which access was mainly by muddy footpaths. Built of iron with a small spire, it was dedicated in April 1895; moves were immediately taken to raise funds for the permanent church. W. D. Caröe, architect to the Ecclesiastical Commissioners, undertook the design. Despite numerous financial difficulties, with planning conditions and with the site, work started late in 1900 by a Kilburn builder. The first part of the church was dedicated on 12 October 1901 by Bishop Winnington-Ingram—the first consecration at which he officiated after his appointment to the See of London. Completion of the nave took another five years to effect.

St Anne's, Salusbury Road, started as a mission church in 1900, serving the Queen's Park estate on the western side of the road. The permanent building, consisting simply of nave, chancel, aisles and a chapel, was designed by J. E. K and J. P. Cutts and opened in 1905.

St Lawrence, Chevening Road, also designed by the Cutts, in 1906, was a fine small church in Early English Gothic style; it became redundant

in the 1970s, was demolished and replaced by an attractive block of council flats, to which the name of the former church was given.

In the territory behind Cricklewood Broadway, hard by the eastern end of Gladstone Park, is St Michael's parish and its church. The area was undeveloped until the late 1890s when the fields of the local farms—Sherrick Green, Lower Oxgate and Baker's—began to become water-logged building sites. In 1904 the New River Water Company (later the Metropolitan Water Board and now Thames Water Authority) built its pumping station near the Acton branch line. There was a garage and work-shop in Langton Road belonging to the London Power Omnibus Company (the LGOC had their garage a few hundred yards up the Edgware Road beyond the railway bridge which is now London Transport's Cricklewood Garage). Mr. L. O. Waller owned a botanical nursery near the top of Mora Road. W. J. Fowler had a printing works originally in one of the new houses in Pine Road and then in Cricklewood Broadway.

In the midst of—and perhaps because of—this activity, St Michael's parish, formed in 1907, began religious services in a mission church near the Mora Road Council Schools under the Rev. T. D. Lloyd whose vigour and energy soon led to the decision to build a permanent church. J. S. Alder was named as architect and in July 1910 it was consecrated by the Bishop of London, Dr. Winnington-Ingram. Mr. Ivor Bulmer-Thomas has said

> If the Church of St. Michael lay at the junction of the Edgware Road and the North Circular Road instead of being in a quiet backwater ... it would be universally known as one of the finest modern buildings in North London ... True, the church that rose to Alder's designs in 1909-10 still lacks the noble tower that he conceived ... but even as it stands, it is a finely planned and finely-executed building, a lovely and satisfying whole.

A mission church under All Souls', Harlesden, was dedicated at the other end of the parish at the corner of Bathurst Gardens and All Souls' Avenue in 1903. This part of Harlesden began to develop in the early years of the century (Holland Road, Wrottesley Road and so on). Steps were taken to build a permanent church and J. S. Alder was selected as architect. In 1914 St Mark's was completed up to the west end which had to be left unattractively covered in corrugated iron until 1968 when it was finished in fine style by Riley and Glanfield. The consecration of the original building was performed by Dr. Winnington-Ingram.

At Neasden, J. S. Alder designed the third of his Willesden churches in 1915. The Rev. Ayerst became vicar of Neasden-cum-Kingsbury in 1898; he was the visionary who worked for the provision of a permanent church at the Neasden end of the parish. A temporary building was opened in 1901 at the corner of Prout Grove and Neasden Lane on land given by Mr. W. E. Nicol of Neasden House and named St Catherine's in honour of his wife (confusingly, Catherine Prout Nicol's mother was from the Nicoll family of Neasden. W. E. Nicol came from Ballogie in Scotland. J. S. Alder designed this church in decorated Gothic style, red brick with stone facings. It was consecrated by Bishop Winnington-Ingram in the midst of the First World War on 4 March 1916. The west front was finished in 1954 by an architect with other Willesden connections, E. B. Glanfield.

St Francis of Assisi at the corner of Ellesmere and Cullingworth Roads had started as a temporary building in 1911 and was rebuilt in yellow stock brick in 1933. As a result of the fluctuation in the communicant population it is now linked with St Andrew's in Willesden Green High Road.

The modern-style church of St Paul's Oxgate was again an instance of a temporary building (1925) being replaced by N. F. Cachemaille-Day's handsome church in 1939. Sadly, it was closed as redundant, after what may be one of the shorter 'lives' of any church in England.

Thus, the expansion of Willesden as a major suburb of London was accompanied by the

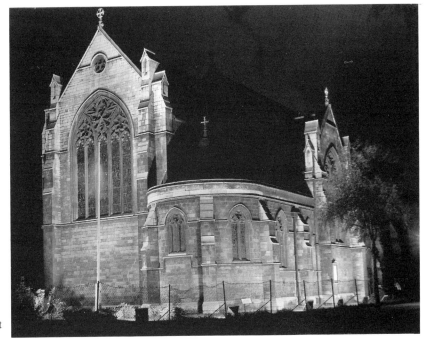

82. St Michael's church, Cricklewood, shown floodlit by G.E.C. in 1960.

provision of some of the essential institutions without which a community cannot thrive.

Schools—Early Days

The churches reacted to the growing population in another traditional way—by having schools attached to their church. In the 1870s they provided St John's school in Kensal Rise and another for the church of the same name at Kilburn; one at All Souls', Harlesden; another at Holy Trinity, Kilburn, St Luke's, Kilburn and St Augustine's—the needs of the Kilburn area were evident. There was also a Roman Catholic school in Peel Road. None of these now exists except the last-named (which has become St Mary's in Canterbury Road). Even so, the provision was not enough to meet the growing young population and further action was needed.

The Willesden Local Board came into dispute with the government's Board for Education about the responsibility for providing additional school places which by the 1880s were clearly needed. Eventually a local School Board was set up and in 1885 opened its first school in Harlesden, moving to Acton Lane in 1891 (it later became known as Harlesden primary school). The site had been bought from the Tubbs family. St Cecilia's church, which stood at the corner, opposite Baker Road, was named after Cecilia Tubbs.

Meanwhile, the Church of England had continued its own expansion and to this period we owe Brondesbury (Christ Church), Keble Memorial, Princess Frederica, and Gordon Memorial elementary schools—the last-named having closed. These last three were built as a result of the drive of Emily Ayekbourn, founder of the Church Extension Association in the 1860s. After moving to Kilburn she helped to raise funds for these and other schools in neighbouring districts. Gordon Memorial was named after General Gordon of Khartoum; Princess Frederica was a cousin of Queen Victoria. Christ Church school was founded by Dr. Williams, rector of the parent church at Brondesbury, originally in houses near the *Prince of Wales* public house in Willesden Lane and then in purpose-built premises in Clarence Road, which opened in 1889. The Roman Catholic diocese responded to the growth of the Harlesden part of Willesden and opened an elementary school in Park Parade (St Joseph's) and, attached to the Convent of Jesus and Mary, a secondary school which for a time also took in boarders.

The Education Act of 1902 swept away the School Boards, made the new counties, like Middlesex, the Education Authority for the area. Part III of the Act allowed districts like Willesden to set up an Education Committee for Elementary education.

83. Interior of Kilburn Grammar School.

In 1912, a census of Willesden schools showed that there were 28,973 elementary school-children and 2,871 in non-elementary schools.

Meanwhile, day secondary schools had begun to appear in the area. Mrs. Maria Grey founded a college for training secondary teachers in Bishopsgate in 1876. After several moves it transferred to Willesden in 1894, on a site in The Avenue. A girls' school, Brondesbury and Kilburn High, was opened at about the same time in Salusbury Road in response to the growing demand for improved education for girls. It proved to be a school with a good record in education; among its pupils were the model 'Twiggy' (Lesley Hornby) and Gwen Molloy.

Kilburn Grammar School for Boys originated in 1898 in premises at 1 Willesden Lane 'for the sons of business and professional men'. It also experienced several moves before its eventual home was established in Salusbury Road. Its first Head was Dr. Bonavia Hunt (later Chairman of the Willesden School Board) and its patron was the then Bishop of London, Dr. Mandell Creighton, after whom the school hall was named. The school has had quite a distinguished role to play in local affairs, although one of its best-known alumni is Richard Baker of BBC music fame. It has contributed three mayors (including myself); headmasters and others who have made their mark including the author of the earlier book on Willesden, Simeon Potter.

The Catholic Church

Fr. B. Ward was sent by Cardinal Manning in 1885 to minister to the needs of the Catholic communicants in Harlesden. From a house in Tubbs Road the new community moved to an iron-built church in Manor Park Road in 1886 (near the Convent of Jesus and Mary). A new statue of Our Lady of Willesden was carved from the wood of an oak which had overlooked the pre-

Reformation shrine at St Mary's. A permanent church was built in Crownhill Road on a portion of convent property and opened by Cardinal Bourne in 1907 who also opened the larger replacement church of Our Lady of Willesden in Nicoll Road in 1931. Designed by W. C. Mangan, the church is built of red brick, has semi-circular east and west ends with impressive vaulting and a feeling of great size.

St Mary's and St Andrew's church stands on Dollis Hill—indeed its lower level, where the hall was constructed, had to be dug out of the hillside. The Institute of Charity supported St Andrew's Hospital from 1915 and was asked in 1929 to take over the new Dollis Hill parish. Fr. John Keatinge organised the building of the church which opened in 1933 and which was in the grounds of the house of the Vicar-General of Westminster, Father Carton de Wiart. On the gates at both ends of the church frontage can be seen the date 1911 when his house was built. The church is attractively built in red brick with Greek-style broken pediments and a contrasting semi-circular window between the upper and lower levels.

St Patrick's on the new St Raphael's estate complex with community hall, St Mary Magdalen,

imposing on Willesden Green hill and the Five Precious Wounds, four-square in Stonebridge near its Anglican counterpart, St Michael's, complete the Catholic circle of churches.

The Jewish Community

The Jewish community of Willesden has waxed and waned over the last century. In Judaism a minyan (a quorum of 10 confirmed males) can hold services anywhere, but a larger congregation inevitably seeks permanent premises. Thus it came about that a meeting of Jewish residents of Kilburn and Brondesbury at the 'Restormel' home of Solomon Barnett in October 1900 decided to build a synagogue. A site in Chevening Road owned by Mr. Barnett was sold by him to the Trustees below cost price. While a temporary building was being erected, use was made of Kilburn Grammar School's hall. Fund-raising went on apace to good effect. On 9 April 1905, Brondesbury Synagogue, the first in Willesden, was opened by Sir Marcus Samuel (later Lord Bearsted) and Lionel de Rothschild. The building is rectangular in shape and built of red brick. It has two rectangular towers, five moorish-style arches and a large ladies' gallery giving a lofty, spacious and impressive aspect. The slope of the hill allowed a large hall to be constructed beneath the Synagogue itself. It was shamefully attacked by vandals and burnt in 1966. Although it was speedily rehabilitated and re-opened, this disaster and the decline in the Jewish population of the district led to its being closed for religious purposes—the first to open, and the first to close. Subsequently, in 1975, Brent council acquired it for use by Brondesbury and Kilburn High School and as a community centre. It was later sold to a Muslim school.

Cricklewood Synagogue began in the 1920s and the new congregation pressed on with fund-raising for its permanent building so well that, in September 1930, the Chief Rabbi, Dr. Hertz, laid the foundation stone at a ceremony at which the chairman of Willesden council (Miss Royle) was also among the distinguished guests. Designed by C. J. Eprile, it is a handsome brick and Portland stone cement building, square in plan with accommodation for about 100 worshippers. It was the first synagogue to be built on the cantilever principle, without piers supporting the ladies' gallery. The roof of structural steel is a special type of construction. There is an impressive display of stained glass windows on Jewish themes, all by David Hillman. The completed building was opened on 28 June 1931. It served the fast growing community of German refugees in the years after it opened. However, by the 1980s the community

84. Our Lady of Willesden Roman Catholic church, pictured in 1961.

85. *(Above)* Brondesbury synagogue, the first in Willesden. It is now part of a Moslem school.

86. *(Left)* Cricklewood synagogue in 1960. It has now been converted into flats.

had shrunk and the synagogue, minus its stained glass windows, was converted into flats.

Willesden Synagogue at Heathfield Park was built in 1937 by one of the smaller groups, the Federation of Synagogues, but funds ran out; it was taken over by the main body, United Synagogues, who closed down their smaller institution in College Road, Kensal Rise. (The author's marriage was solemnised there in 1944 following a civil ceremony in October 1943 at Willesden Register Office.)

Dollis Hill Synagogue began in 1929, meeting at first in local halls. Funds were raised for a permanent building and the foundation stone of the 'Gladstone Park and Neasden Synagogue' in Clifford Way was laid in June 1931, the service conducted by Dayan M. Gollop. This synagogue continues to serve its locality. A new congregation began to meet in Park Avenue and in houses in the locality. In 1933 the Dollis Hill Synagogue was founded at Park Side, in the building now known as the Joseph Freedman Hall. The present building was consecrated in February 1938 by the Chief Rabbi Dr. J. H. Hertz in the presence of the mayor of Willesden. It was designed by Sir Owen Williams (who built the Empire Pool) and is of reinforced concrete. It is now a listed building. On 29 December 1946, having successfully survived the war, an outrageous act of vandalism was perpetrated in the synagogue.

The Nonconformist Churches
In 1820 the vestry minutes of St Mary's, Willesden, recorded 'there has lately been erected in the parish a Dissenting Meeting House tending to cause religious divisions among them and which they fear is chiefly to be attributed to the want of Divine Service at the Parish Church'. The brief history concerns a Mr. Nodes who used to visit his mother in a cottage at the junction of Willesden Green High Road and Dudden Hill Lane (opposite where now are the *Case is Altered* and the Salvation Army Citadel). Every Sunday, as Potter tells us, he visited her to read her sermons; a small congregation assembled and a chapel was built, giving rise to the name Chapel End. It was pulled down in 1908 for road widening; and the little Metro Cinema was built on the neighbouring site.

Methodism in Harlesden dates back at least as far as 1847. It seems that there was even a church building, possibly on the present site which, thanks to a Mr. Harman, was retained by the church. The 'new' church was built in 1869 as the Willesden Wesleyan Methodist church at a cost of £1,500, together with a Sunday and a day school (the latter, however, closed within 10 years). In 1882 a replacement was built for nearly four times the original cost. It had a tall spire and was built in red brick with white stone banding. Every Saturday evening at this time a popular temperance entertainment was held (½d. for a cup of tea and ½d. for a piece of cake). A hall was built in Tavistock Road in 1906 and the church's name was changed to 'Harlesden'. Over the years, church and residents each complained about 'noise' from open air services and from passing bands and trams! The Second World War damaged the church beyond repair and it was not until 1956 that the new church was built. It is set back from the building line in Harlesden High Street and constructed in a well-designed, handsome, modern style in yellow brick. In recent years, reacting to

the change in the population and sensitive to the needs of the 'inner city' area, the church has become very closely involved with the community, a large proportion of which is now West Indian.

Primitive Methodists and Wesleyan Methodists both had their adherents. Others have come and some have gone—a small chapel in the Harrow Road later became the Moonshine Community Arts Workshop. On Neasden Lane another church went the same way as the one in Neasden—sold and demolished to make way for a smaller building and a commercial development—in this case housing. Kensal Rise had welcomed Methodists since at least 1886; their imposing church was built in 1900 in Chamberlayne Road.

The Baptists had a number of solidly-constructed edifices including the elegant West Kilburn chapel (which is protected within the total redevelopment of the area) and at Willesden Green where after a series of temporary locations the present building with tower and gothic aspect was erected. The district was well-served by Baptist foundations in Cricklewood, Harlesden and Kensal Rise.

In 1972 the Presbyterian and Congregational churches made ecumenical progress and came together as the United Reform church. One of the early foundations was Willesden Presbyterian church (St Margaret's), a solid gothic building at the corner of Nicoll Road and Craven Park Road. It began in 1874 at the start of the development of Harlesden when it was still a village. A few men had met together at Harley Lodge, Stonebridge Park in May 1873, raised money to build a hall and this, in turn, led to the impulse to construct the church which was completed in 1876. From this beginning, mission work extended to railway workers (a Railway Institute was built in 1878) and an offshoot of the church established in College Park. Willesden Presbyterian church was renamed St Margaret's in 1959 and, after the union, joined with St George's Moravian church, Willesden Lane.

Cricklewood Congregational church began in the 1880s on the Hampstead side of Edgware Road; the district was still rural. The Lown Memorial Hall was used until 1902 when the brick building with turreted tower and gothic arches was opened. Beneath the church, a hall was opened a year later by their 'neighbour' Lord Aberdeen of Dollis Hill House, and named after him. During the First World War, Lown Hall was used as a hostel for Belgian refugees and more recently as a youth club. With the change in population, the church closed in the 1970s and was sold to become an Islamic Centre.

87. Harlesden Wesleyan Methodist church, *c.*1900.

88. The Congregational church in Chichele Road, 1905. It is now a mosque.

The Congregational church in Church Road is described by Pevsner as free Gothic of 1900 with a nice asymmetrical south-west tower and spirelet by Spalding and Spalding. Members contributed to the support of the military hospital at Dollis Hill during the First World War. A War Memorial Hall was built in 1924 and later, when the church itself was let to a film company, it was used for worship.

A New Variety of Faiths
Religious belief is not confined to major organised religions. Brent contains a wide variety of other congregations—including Seventh Day Adventists, a Russian Orthodox Convent in Brondesbury Park, Latter Day Saints (Mormons),

Spiritualists, the Church of the Transfiguration (in a former Methodist Church), a Welsh chapel in Willesden Lane Gospel halls and the Salvation Army. More recently Pentecostal churches catering for the needs of the West Indian community have taken over many former chapels and halls.

The Islamic faith provides for its adherents in the familiar way—at first in houses—and then in purpose-built mosques. In the meantime, a former chapel has been converted into a Mosque and Islamic Centre in Chichele Road. The Hindu faiths have also been providing opportunities for their adherents to worship. A large centre was established in Stonebridge (Meadow Garth) and a magnificent Swaminarayan temple has been erected in Willesden Lane.

Chapter 14

Democracy Rules: The New District Council

First Elections

The Local Government Act of 1888 provided for local self-government—county councils and district councils. Willesden applied to become a District Council. Out of the old Middlesex were created the new Middlesex and the London County Councils (the latter with parts of Essex, Kent and Surrey also; the area was based on the already out-of-date 1855 boundary of the Metropolitan Board of Works—thus Willesden escaped the net of the LCC).

The parliamentary electorate in the district in November 1894 (which was part of the Harrow Division) was:

Willesden	16,815
Kingsbury	140
Wembley	665

In June 1894, the triennial election of the Willesden School Board (untouched by local government reform) had produced a sensational result—the Progressives and Labour factions nearly won a majority, gaining three to take four of the nine seats—the others going to the Voluntarists (or supporters of denominational schools). It presaged a hard fought battle for Willesden District Council at the end of the year. And so it proved.

The number of seats on the new Willesden council was 21 in seven wards compared with 15 in four wards of the old Local Board; there were 51 candidates.

Party politics entered in by proxy and suggestion only. Colonel Charles Pinkham was well known in Conservative circles but his public advertisement, with Dr. Crone and Mr. Toley, thanking electors when they were nominated and returned unopposed for Kensal Green, made no mention of political affiliations. Biddiscombe, Goldsmith and Watson, three of the unsuccessful candidates in Willesden Green, stood under the banner of the Rate-payers' Association and a number of others were also supported by their local branch. A small number stood, boldly but unsuccessfully, as Labour candidates—they included Albert Hodges, a joiner in Willesden

Green Ward, and Charles Catt in Church End, although the newspapers carefully avoided describing the interest in which they stood!

About half the new council were old Board members including the longest serving, James Stewart, elected for South Kilburn (together with W. B. Luke—a Liberal, and J. Birt). He had been chairman of the Board since 1888 and was elected to preside over the new council for the first term.

Willesden's Growing Pains

The late Mr. Harry Wallis of Kensal Green was born in 1885 in Harlesden and started work at the age of fourteen. Harlesden Road was almost a footpath between fields.

He told me that Kensal Green was known for a period as the 'Greyhound Estate, College Park', after the first road built there. The difference in building styles between the earlier houses and those which came later is marked. There was a milestone in Harrow Road, opposite St John's Church, near the *Plough*. To the north of the church was the LGOC horse-bus depot from which yellow buses served the route from Kensal Rise to London Bridge.

The building methods were similar to those in other parts of London—few large scale contractors were involved; owners' land was divided into plots. A jobbing builder, or a carpenter, bricklayer or other tradesman, would borrow money from the banks. Too often this became a device to seize land, as foreclosure was frequently imposed and the poor builder might lose £60 or so, and his limited expectations.

Mr. Wallis claimed that some of Kensal Green was open common land in his youth—this probably referred to the land near Wakeman's Road and on the north side of the railway where the fields were not built on until later in the 1890s. In 1911 the parish of St Martin's, Kensal Rise, had a population of about 10,000—mixed from 'the very poor who when thrown out of work by weather and so on have little or nothing to fall back on, to those who have regular employment as clerks,

89. Willesden District Council Officers' Club *c*.1900, dressed in their best.

90. Kensal Rise, Chamberlayne Road, looking north, *c*.1910.

accountants, salesmen, etc. in the City'. In February and March 1934, shelter was given to the Jarrow marchers in the Long Room behind the church—a demonstration of modern Christianity at work.

Bannister's Farm on the north side of Kilburn Lane was linked by a hump-backed bridge to the fields north of the North London Railway. The field paths had stiles and kissing-gates. Beyond Kensal Rise station, the road petered out into a farm track.

A friendly, well-researched article in the journal *London* of 16 April 1896 says:

> Willesden today, with nearly 90,000 people within it boundaries, is practically only twenty years old [compare the growth of the New Towns in the years after the second World War]. It was an insignificant district, with a small population until the Local Board was formed in 1875. Since then it has grown remarkably year after year ... And yet the district is by no means covered, or is likely to be, for years ... by far the greater part of Willesden remains rural. Willesden, indeed, comprises a series of hamlets.
>
> At present, most of these hamlets (sic) stand isolated, and form pleasant rural abodes, but the streets and houses show persistency in creeping towards each other.

In the early years of the century, Wembley became displeased with a nuisance emanating from Willesden's sewage farm at Stonebridge and legal proceedings were started. The smell from the site was said, by one member of the Wembley council, to have been one of the reasons why his district developed later than the surrounding areas.

In July 1896 Greenford council applied to the High Court for an injunction against Willesden for allowing sewage to flow into the Brent from the sewage farm. The injunction was granted but suspended for several months to allow Willesden—meaning Oscar Robson—time to proceed with its sewage scheme, which were to cost nearly twenty thousand pounds. A further step was taken in 1908 when 'the greatest scheme in Willesden's history' was effected at a cost of £150,000 to dispose of sewage through the LCC sewers. This was quoted as a satisfactory solution to a serious problem.

When the new Urban District Council took over control, Willesden was already a large-sized town—and was still the fastest-growing in Middlesex. Yet, there were large tracts of undeveloped land. The members of the council grappled with huge problems. Within a few years they were seeking to become a borough so as to exercise greater powers as well as to enjoy

91. Dr. J. S. Crone, a much-loved G.P. and long-serving councillor.

enhanced status, but this did not materialise for another 30 years. However, an enlargement of the membership of the council was agreed by the Local Government Board but even this took time to develop, consider and agree. The new 33-man council was first elected in 1907.

During these early years of the 20th century, the dominant personalities included Dr. J. S. Crone, a charming Irish physician who was described (in an obituary in the *Kilburn Times*) as having 'unquestionable ability, undoubted impartiality and unbounded popularity'. His fellow-councillor from Kensal Rise was Charles Pinkham who attained almost every honour a locality can offer—chairman of the district council, county councillor, M.P. and a knighthood for his services to the community. Strangely enough, while Dr. Crone is remembered in Crone Court, Denmark Road, South Kilburn, Pinkham's memorial is outside the borough on a section of the North Circular Road. (Just to confuse everyone there was another councillor, W. J. Pincombe, who served with some distinction including chairing the education committee.) Charles

92. Harvist Road school (now Kensal Rise primary), *c*.1910.

93. Furness Road school, *c*.1905. The school was bombed during the Second World War.

93. Stonebridge (Park) schools, c.1900. The building was designed by G. E. Laurence for the Willesden School Board.

Pinkham was said to have a very hearty and convincing manner; a man who did not talk much but was listened to and 'no wonder, for he goes straight to the point, no high-falutin' or superfluous words, but a sort of manner that makes you feel sure of his sincerity'.

An unknown poet was quoted in 1894 in lyrical style:

Weary man may sleep serene
In lovely sylvan Willesden Green.

Worthy of Betjeman; were it only true today!

The tremendous pressure of housing development in Willesden in the last quarter of the 19th century eased only slightly. Willesden saw the importance of preserving open parkland as a means of recreation and as a source of fresh air.

In 1907 the last shepherd's dog licence in Willesden was granted. One generation had seen the conversion of rural to urban life. In 1898 Willesden was proclaiming that its rates were, except for two other districts, the lowest in the county at 5s. 3d. in the pound.

This period, up to the First World War, was one of the busiest in school building progress of the whole hundred years from 1875. Leopold was followed by Harvist Road, Stonebridge by Salusbury, Furness and Gibbon; then Mora Road, Oldfield Road and others. The School Board, became an Education Committee in 1903.

Most interesting was the pioneering work under Dr. William Butler, MOH, on medical inspections in schools which led to the 1907 Act of Parliament making this a national scheme. His Report 'Hygienic Control of Public Elementary Schools', despite its prosaic title, is a masterpiece of well-researched policy recommendations.

1904 saw the first Labour member elected to Willesden council—Dave Barrett, for Church End.

One of his early moves was to try to get a 40 per cent increase in street-sweepers' wages, but his more conservative (and liberal) colleagues did not see it in the same light. In 1910 Percy Bond, later one of the major figures in the Willesden Labour Party, was elected together with Herbert Grimwood; Labour candidates won four out of six seats contested and in 1913 eight out of nine, but it was until not 1934 that Labour won its first majority council in Willesden.

Housing the Masses

Barry Pain, the Cockney poet, wrote, at about the turn of the century:

The City's growed
The country lane's a wood-paved road,
And still ole Lunnon's awms stretch art
And grab the plices rahnd abart.

In 1901 Willesden's population was 114,821, living in 16,045 houses; its expansion, south of the Metropolitan Railway line was almost complete.

Many solid mansions of the middle class merchants, annuitants, widows and retired officers have survived in Willesden. Working class houses fell prey to mid-20th-century redevelopment in Stonebridge, South Kilburn and Church End. Thus we still have villas like Vernon House in Willesden Lane, once the borough's education offices and then a school.

Willesden saw an expansion in the 20 years following the formation of the district council almost as dramatic as in the previous twenty. In fact, by 1911, it reached 154,214. The result of these developments was to leave an oval of open land from Willesden cemetery to Brondesbury House while virtually all the land north from Gladstone Park was still virgin farm land. Here the Willesden paddocks offered a centre for horses renowned throughout the country (it belonged to and was built by the Tattersall family before 1841) matched by the stud farm at Neasden. Oxgate Farm was evident, alongside other farms, on the Dollis Hill slopes.

The development of Queen's Park Estate, on the site of the once famous Royal Agricultural show, belongs to this period. This was part of the church lands belonging originally to the Prebendaries of St Paul's—some of whom are commemorated in the road names—Peploe and Kempe. Keslake was one of the builders of the estate. Creighton Road (named after Bishop Mandell Creighton who was closely associated with the early Kilburn Grammar School) was originally Sinclair Road after another church dignitary. Milman Road commemorated Henry

95. Willesden Paddocks—
Tattersalls. The stallions'
boxes in 1841.

96. Willesden Lane, near
Deerhurst Road in 1910.

Hart Milman (1791-1868), a poet and historian of some distinction in his lifetime; he became Dean of St Paul's. Harvist Road, of course, commemorates the brewer, Edward Harvist, whose benefactions for road maintenance and generally for the benefit of the people of the borough are still going strong. Chevening Road is, also, connected with the church—it was the home (near Sevenoaks) of the one-time chairman of the Ecclesiastical Commissioners, Lord Stanhope. The origins of the road names on the east side of Queen's Park are not readily identifiable.

Cricklewood was opened up around the turn of the century. George Furness and his family were involved in developing the area north of George Howard's older Oaklands Estate. The prosaic tree names of Olive, Agave, Mora, Larch and Pine are supplemented by Hassop Road, the Derbyshire village from whence the Furness family originated (near Longstone village where George Furness was born and, coincidentally, a few miles from Chatsworth). A separate small development relates to Lord Temple who had seats at Wotton House near Aylesbury and at Newton Park near Bath—hence Temple, Wotton and Newton Roads. The shape of the original estates on which these developments were built can be clearly identified.

Prominent in the development of Willesden from the 1890s was the architect and surveyor, George A. Sexton, assisted later by his son, G. W. F. Sexton. The older Sexton was chairman of Willesden UDC, 1903-6 and 1923-24. Among

97. The field, Brondesbury, in 1894. It was near Mapesbury and Exeter Roads.

98. Willesden Green High Road, c.1910 looking east, with the library on the right.

the buildings and estates with which they were associated were the warehouses for Harvey, Bradfield and Toyer (Bradfield, like Sexton the younger, was at Kilburn Grammar School) at Coombe Road (having previously been in Rucklidge Avenue); garages for Jack Hobbs (who also served on Willesden council) on Willesden Lane and others in South Kilburn and Willesden Green; Rutland Park Mansions; and the houses opposite in Walm Lane which were converted into shops; Foresters' Hall; Wallen's Dairy in Albert Road; Willesden Green Working Men's Club and Kensal Rise Constitutional Club (catholic in approach!) and a laundry in Barretts Green Road. This fine catalogue of work across Willesden, and extending into Alperton, is worthy of wider recognition.

On the Mapesbury Estate, apart from the spine road named after the manor house itself, it is obvious that the streets, which date from the Edwardian period, have Devonian connections—Dartmouth, Dawlish and Teignmouth: Chatsworth, although in Derbyshire, may not be out of place as it is the name of the seat of the Duke of Devonshire. (It has been suggested to me by Mr. G. W. F. Sexton, that the influx of Devon craftsmen into the area may have been the source of these names; and it may be mentioned that Charles Pinkham was a Devonian. The link could be the Duke of Devonshire at the turn of the century who was a prominent Conservative politician.)

White Hall at the corner of Dartmouth and Mapesbury Roads, bearing the date 1905, has a

distinctive style of red bricks and whitewashed walls with timber beams at roof level. There are many other fine houses on the Mapesbury Estate, reflecting similar good taste.

By 1908, the eastern part of Harlesden, towards Kensal Rise, was also largely completed. The brick or stone pillars of the bay windows, gables and tiled roofs testify to the period of construction. These houses were built partly on All Souls' land as the road names testify—Bathurst (a College benefactor); Buchanan, Ridley and Bramston (all Fellows of the Colleges and also politicians); Holland (a fellow and legal expert); Monson (yet another fellow and a diplomat) and Lushington (fellow and a judge): a catalogue of respectable but long-forgotten dignitaries who had no specific connection with Willesden.

Stonebridge, part of the Brett estate, was developed in the last years of the old century; the name Poets' Corner was given to the area from the choice of street names such as Shakespeare, Milton and Shelley—and Carlyle who was almost equally famous as a writer though hardly qualified as a poet. Most of this area was redeveloped in the 1970s although some of the names have been retained.

Willesden once had some of the characteristics of a frontier town as it burst out from London. By the time Edward VII came to the throne, it was a bustling suburb—sometimes pretentious, sometimes fashionable—but alive.

Chapter 15

On the Line

Trains, Trams and Buses

Sir Henry Oakley, one of the leading figures in the development of the electric underground in the latter years of the last century, said in 1899 that the country north of Cricklewood was 'not simply ripe but almost bursting with ripeness for development'. He spoke in support of the proposed North West London Railway which was approved by Parliament but, like many others, was never built. Another ill-fated project would have cut across Willesden and Wembley from Alperton via Neasden to Cricklewood.

The last major new lines to be built in this area were the Great Central extension and the Ealing and South Harrow Line (which initially became part of the District Railway; the route was eventually transferred to the Piccadilly line).

In 1901, the Royal Agricultural Society came back to Willesden leasing nearly 120 acres in Twyford, between the Canal and the new G.W.R. Line to Northolt. It was intended to establish a permanent site for its annual shows. The Prince of Wales (later King George V) opened a railway station on 25 May 1903 and gave the area its new name—Park Royal. The new Ealing and South Harrow Branch of the District Railway first ran to the show with its own Park Royal station (a little distance from the present station) in June of that year.

Unfortunately, not only did bad weather spoil the opening, causing poor attendances, but matters were no better in the next two years and the Society abandoned the site. It was sold (thankfully) by the Royal Agricultural Society for £28,000 to Park Royal estates company. A reminder of the site is *The Plumes* public house. An arrangement was made for a period for it to be used by Queens Park Rangers Football Club. It was then used for military purposes in the First World War. In the 1930s Guinness acquired part of the site for a brewery.

99. The Royal Agricultural Show building at Park Royal, 1904-5. This photograph shows the entrance prior to demolition in 1961.

100. Cricklewood Broadway with the Coronation Clock, *c.*1912. During the 1940s the Clock disappeared in order to 'help the war effort'.

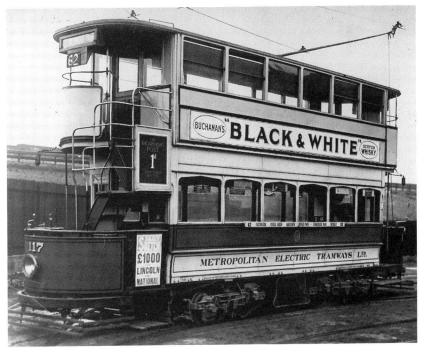

101. The no.62 tram ran along the length of the Harrow Road to Wembley.

Electrification of the Metropolitan Railway was running parallel to that of the District and the older railway beat its younger off-shoot by a few months. A generating station was built at Neasden. First services commenced on 1 January 1905.

A Royal Commission on London Traffic in 1905 declared that trams were 'the most efficient and cheapest means of street conveyance'. This was not a view shared by all members of the Willesden council or the LCC. An alternative proposal by the Royal Commission was a new tube line under the Edgware Road from Cricklewood to Marble Arch. Although this idea has been repeatedly retrieved from the dustbin of history, it has never obtained approval and perhaps never will.

Electric trams, having been successfully demonstrated in America in the 1880s and then in Bristol, first operated in London in the Uxbridge Road in April 1901. Efforts to bring tramways to Willesden met with strong local opposition to proposals by private enterprise (such as North Met Tramways) by the council or by the LCC. Indeed some long-serving members lost their seats on the council in 1901 because of their support. However, progress was unstoppable. The first service in our own area, operated by Metropolitan Electric Tramways (MET), was along the Edgware Road from the *Crown* at Cricklewood to Edgware in December 1904—the LCC refused to allow these trams within their territory and so no southward extension was ever made. In 1906, another MET route along Harrow Road from Paddington to the *Royal Oak,* Harlesden and on to a depot opened at Stonebridge.

This was followed by a line from Harlesden to Stonebridge Park in 1906, extended to Wembley station in April 1908 and to the *Swan* at Sudbury in December 1910.

The Edgware route along Chichele Road was extended in 1906. The route via Church Road to Cricklewood was opened in 1907, linking up at Willesden Green. A few months earlier, the Harlesden route had been extended east to the *Prince of Wales* at Paddington. A last section was from Harlesden to Acton, opened in 1909—providing a bare skeleton of services on some of the main roads in the borough. Nonetheless, tramways provided a cheap, fairly comfortable and popular means of transport—until their unavoidable rigidity of movement clashed with the mobility of cars and forced a move to the more flexible trolley-bus.

A local resident, Mr. L. P. Walter, remembers a light green single-decker motor bus in 1905 from the *Crown* to town which was mechanically unreliable; it was followed by the Straker Squire

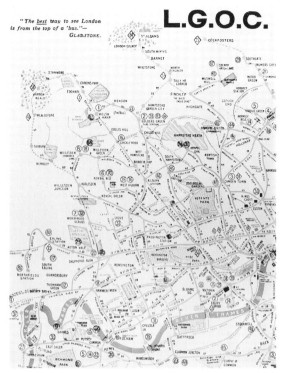

102. This LGOC Motor bus map dates from 1912 and until quite recently many of the route numbers had hardly changed.

bus operated by LMOC under the name Vanguard (one of the largest companies outside the LGOC—The 'General'). The fare to Victoria was 3d. Although a number of companies were in the field for the lucrative commuter traffic (as we now term it) the London General Omnibus Company bought up two of its main rivals in 1908.

In 1912, a route map with the slogan 'Travel above ground—we carry you all the way' has some still familiar information. A no.18 bus travels up the Harrow Road; the no.16 is on its familiar run from Cricklewood to Victoria. The no.6 starts at Kensal Rise for east London and the no.70 and the no.36 from the *Falcon*, West Kilburn.

The L.N.W.R. had obtained an Act in 1907 to build a suburban railway line to Watford. It reached agreement with the Bakerloo for that line to be extended from Paddington to surface at Queen's Park and then proceed by the new line out to Watford. The compulsory powers to acquire land included, for example, portions of Claremont and Albert Roads in Willesden. Two contracts were let to Monk and from Newall and to Naylor Bros. (both engineering firms the north of England) between Willesden and Harrow at a cost of over £110,000. The Bakerloo service began operating

103. Walm Lane, *c*.1912,
with an unexpected no.46
bus.

104. An LGOC no.8 bus being inspected by King George V in 1920.

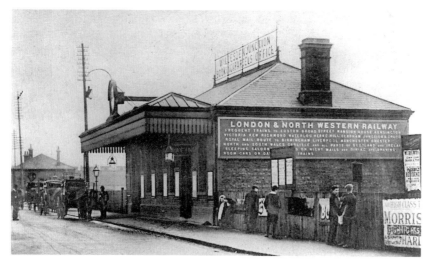

105. Willesden Junction station, *c.*1900 with horse cabs waiting for fares.

overground to Willesden in May 1915 and to Watford in April two years later. The route included a 'fly-under' to bring the line from the eastern to the western side of the main line tracks between Stonebridge Park and Wembley stations. At about the same time, the North London line was electrified and electric trains were able to run from Watford through Wembley (for Sudbury) and Willesden to Broad Street.

Power and Telephones
One of the council's big achievements was the decision to bring electricity into Willesden. Several private companies wanted to undertake the job but Pinkham persuaded the council to set up its own scheme and an engineer, E. T. R. Murray, was appointed in 1898 (he was the son of the editor of the *Oxford Dictionary*). A site for the generating station was found at Lower Place but it was decided later that Taylor's Lane would be better. It was built in 1903. The scheme went ahead but a change of policy led to a deal with the North Met Electricity Supply Company—a unique commercial agreement—to sell the undertaking to them and for the council to buy back the supply in bulk. Electric street lighting commenced in June 1903 in Harlesden and Church End. The new lighting spread rapidly through the shopping districts and factories and then to the houses, rendering the lamplighter redundant. Willesden electricity ultimately succumbed to nationalisation in 1948.

The early development of the telephone in this country, was by private companies, by municipalities (of which Hull is the only one remaining) and then by the Post Office which gradually absorbed all the others. The first exchanges, in London, were opened in 1879. One

of the last major private companies, the National Telephone Company, was absorbed into the Post Office on 1 January 1912.

Thus it happened that, for a short period, there were two networks in this area. The National had exchanges for Harlesden (1896), Harrow (1901), Ealing (1895) and Hampstead (1900). The Post Office exchanges were at Harrow, Ealing (both 1903), Hampstead (1904) and in, or shortly after, 1907—Wembley and Kingsbury. Willesden's exchange in St Andrew's Road was opened in October 1901.

Many of the earliest phones were in public call boxes such as in Luke Fowler's shop at 201 Church Road, Willesden, at various post offices and railway stations.

Wires were, for obvious reasons, carried above ground on poles that are still to be found in parts of Willesden. The Post Office, however, negotiated many way-leaves to allow for underground cables.

The Local Press
Kilburn acquired its own paper in March 1868 when R. G. Bassett, a young printer aged 26, hand-printed the eight-page *Kilburn Times* at 5 Park Place, Carlton Road (i.e. Carlton Vale). Its front page advertisements were full of appeals to purchase the 'cheapest house' or at 'the lowest possible prices'. Rogers the baker offered to wait on customers daily while the insurance advertisement was more attuned to the professional man.

Within a few years the paper was taken over by another printer, Thomas Smith, who, as proprietor and editor for over 36 years, left an indelible impression on the *Kilburn Times*. At one time he also served on the Willesden Local

The North West
JEWISH
MIRROR

Circulating in Cricklewood, Brondesbury, Kilburn, Willesden, Dollis Hill, Wembley, Hampstead, Golders Grn., Hendon & St. John's Wood

Vol. II. No. 5.   PRICE 2d.   Friday, 23rd October, 1936.

NEWS from all QUARTERS

BOARD OF DEPUTIES MEETING

A sharp protest against Fascist attempts to identify the Jews in the public mind with

TERRORISTS SENTENCED

Four members of the gang of Sheikh Izz ed Din El K------m, who confessed to the m------ ------geant of P------

CONSUL AIDS ROUMANIAN NAZIS

The ------ M------

106. *The North-West Jewish Mirror*, a local newspaper published by the author's father between 1936-7.

Board—the first but not the last local newspaperman to serve in two roles.

March 1877 saw the start of the *Willesden and Kilburn Chronicle*, published for *Willesden Press Association* by J. M. Houghton at 52 Alpha Terrace, Canterbury Road. The two papers were linked although it was not until 1892 that the formal grouping of the 'North Western Printing and Publishing Association' was established.

Two sons-in-law of Thomas Smith joined the board and a descendant of one of these, Mr. J. M. Page, was closely involved with the paper until the 1980s. Gradually, improvements in the printing arrangements were undertaken—from flat bed to typecasting machines. Photographs appeared occasionally even in the late 1890s but they were not a regular feature until the 1920s.

The *Willesden Citizen*, which offered a Liberal/Radical view of local politics, was published from November 1913 to 1965 (when it was absorbed into the Mercury series). Its publisher, J. M. Whyte, was against gambling, betting and intemperance and his first edition carried a big advertisement of celebrities supporting his campaign against the demon drink.

In April 1936, my father, a professional journalist, ventured into the dangerous waters of publishing and brought out the *North West Jewish Mirror*. Published first from Kilburn High Road and then from Priory Park Road (now the site of Ryde House), it provided a news and feature service for the large Jewish communities of Willesden, Golders Green, Edgware and the rest of the north-west segment of London. It warned strongly against German Nazism and British Fascism, reported on the deteriorating situation between Jews and Arabs in Palestine and announced weddings, the opening of the North London Jewish Boys' Club in Ashford Road and other local news. A budding but frustrated journalist with the initials LS or pseudonym 'N. Lennards' wrote on stamp-collecting. Sadly, it did not maintain its circulation, advertisers began to withdraw support and its last issue went to press exactly a year after the first.

Chapter 16

Mind and Body

Libraries

Libraries are almost as old as civilisation it-self, but until the establishment of municipal libraries under the Public Libraries Act, they were mainly the preserve of a privileged minority in this country. A public library [is] an engine of great potentialities for rational welfare and the essential foundation for progress in education and culture without which no people can hold its own in the struggle for existence.

(*Jubilee History*).

Willesden was too small in 1850 to consider adopting the first Public Libraries Act; even in 1877 there was not sufficient support. A Willesden library and institute was formed in 1890 at 3 Willesden Park Houses (near Willesden Green station) but it lasted barely a year. Support for a public library was organised by W. B. Luke, Liberal member of the Willesden Board and Mr. W. North. By appealing to public opinion, they forced the Board to poll the parish. The proposal recognised the scattered nature of the district and recommended the creation of three branch

libraries. One opponent wrote: 'If public libraries are needed why cannot they be supported by those who need them backed by those philanthropists who wish to provide them?'—a backwoods view, not unknown even today.

The result of the poll was a resounding 2 to 1 majority in favour. A Library Commission was set up in 1891 and went about acquiring sites in Kilburn, Harlesden and Willesden Green. Frank Chennell, aged 21, applied for the post of librar-ian at each and was successful with the latter post. He stayed in the Willesden service until his retirement as borough librarian in 1937. When he started, the libraries were the centres of small urban developments separated by green fields—so that the walk from Willesden Green library to Kilburn was by stile and footpath. John Cash, a Harlesden architect, was responsible for the design of his local library—at the time it was well-provided with trees and bushes, front and back. The other two were put out to competition and Willesden Green was another success for Newman and Newman (they also designed the town hall in Dyne Road and Willesden General Hospital).

107. Park Avenue. In the background the house used as a library during the 1890s may be seen.

108. Willesden Green library, 1910.

109. The opening of Cricklewood library in 1932. The building now also houses the borough archives.

On 30 January 1894 Kilburn library, designed by Edmeston and Gabriel, was opened by the Rev. J. E. C. Weldon, headmaster of Harrow school; there was a stock of about 4,000 volumes. The building was combined with a mortuary and fire-station—one of the first examples of municipal co-operation. Harlesden library was opened by Sir Henry Roscoe, M.P. on 14 February of that year, with a stock of 6,400 books. Willesden Green library was third by a few months, opened on 18 July by I. E. B. Cox, the local M.P., with a stock of 5,000 books; the building cost £2,600.

'Open access' had not yet been invented. Borrowers consulted a catalogue and referred to an indicator to check if the books they wanted were in the library. A specimen of this old-fashioned device may be seen at the Grange Museum.

Kensal Rise now wanted the same service but money was short. All Souls' College generously donated land and a reading room funded by the council was opened by the American humorist Mark Twain (Samuel Langhorne Clemens) on 27 September 1900. Four years later, with the help of a benefaction of £3,000 from Andrew Carnegie, an extension was built to provide a branch library, designed by A. H. Murray-Rust and opened in May 1904.

The new Library Committee in 1921 opened makeshift part-time evening branches at Lower Place, Neasden, South Kilburn, Cricklewood,

Bridge Road and Braintcroft, between 1922 and 1928. These helped to extend the service while permanent buildings were planned. The first of these was at Cricklewood where, again, All Souls' College helped by presenting the site to the council. Designed by the engineer and surveyor, F. G. Wilkinson, it was the first planned open-access library in Willesden.

Next came the branch at Neasden, at Aboyne Road, also designed by Mr. Wilkinson and opened by Sir William Hadow in February 1931. With the opening of these libraries, Willesden was provided with one of the best library services in the county. Books issued in 1930-31 exceeded one million for the first time. It was replaced in 1982 by a new branch in Neasden shopping centre.

In 1937 F. E. Chennell retired after 43 years as a librarian in Willesden but, sad to relate, died within a few months of leaving office. He was succeeded by Mr. George Godding, who had been at Kilburn library since 1894; he, in turn, retired in 1945 to be succeeded by Mr J. G. Gillett who supervised the post-war period and the Brent amalgamation.

The original Willesden Green building was largely demolished in the 1980s to provide a site for a library centre. After a political battle in

Brent council the lovely frontage section was retained as an elegant part of the High Road scene.

Open Spaces

No sooner had Willesden UDC been formed than the councillors bid to rescue some of the rapidly disappearing fields for recreation and leisure for the people.

Behind George Furness' house lay Hunger Fields with the Knowle, or hilltop, on which was, for a period, a bandstand. In 1892 the land was bought for £15,000 to make into Roundwood Park. Originally laid out by Oscar Robson, for about £11,000, many more years of gardeners' toil have been poured into making it one of the loveliest of London's pleasaunces of greenswards and flower beds. It was opened on 11 May 1895 by R. D. M. Little Q.C., chairman of the Middlesex County Council who 'dedicated it for ever to the people'. A portion of the purchase price was contributed by local donations. Oscar Robson made it 'a Garden of Eden without the serpent'.

Dollis Hill House and its grounds were acquired from Sir Hugh Gilzean-Reid who, in turn, had bought it from the Earl of Aberdeen when he became Governor General of Canada in 1897. The then chairman of the council, Charles Pinkham,

110.   Water fountain in Gladstone Park, *c*.1905.

111. Allotments in Kensal Rise, *c*.1905. They were situated between All Souls' Avenue and Chamberlayne Road.

was the leading spirit in the move to bring this essential portion of open space into public ownership. Despite objections from Harlesden residents to Willesden's putting up £30,000 of rate-payers' money (Middlesex and London County Councils between them put up £15,000), the district council agreed and the Local Government Board approved the cost of £50,000. It was properly laid out, though not as extensively as Roundwood Park, under the proposed name 'Dollis Hill Park' although on its opening by Lord Aberdeen, it was named, appropriately, after William Gladstone. A contemporary article described the house:

> Dollis Hill Park with its lilied pool, its fair lawns and noble trees is beautiful enough in itself. From the breezy hill where the house stands the eye wanders away westward over a richly wooded country (i.e. Wembley) south-ward to Willesden, Brondesbury and Kilburn where long rows of brick and mortar are advancing dangerously nearer every day and threaten to cover the whole neighbourhood with an unbroken phalanx of houses. East-ward, the view is bounded by the northern heights of London.

A few years later, the first open-air swimming pool in the area was opened in that same park. The house has, happily, survived and is maintained by the council. During the First World War it became a military hospital and continued to serve as a convalescent home for pensioners after the war.

In 1902 the council tried to buy and preserve as open space the National Athletic Ground in Kensal Rise but failed to meet the price and it fell to developers who carved out Liddell Gardens and other roads nearby. More successful, a few years later, was the acquisition of land off All Souls' Avenue (near Welfords Farm) and this became King Edward's Recreation Ground named in honour of the reigning monarch.

Cemeteries have a special place in the community (technically areas of 'open space'). Leaving aside the vast Kensal Green cemetery on the border of, but outside, the borough, and the Paddington cemetery, which the council took over from Westminster council, there is a small cemetery associated with the original parish church of St Mary's, Willesden's original burial ground. The main cemetery within Willesden is the 50-acre site at Pound Lane—a municipal ground opened in 1893 with Jewish burial lands next door. There is, in addition, a modern cemetery run by Brent at Carpenders Park, which was originally provided by Willesden in place of their formerly intended burial ground in Birchen Grove, Kingsbury (now Brent's parks' nursery).

Allotments are a valuable means of recreation and offering no small value to many hundreds of gardeners and horticulturists. Some 75 acres have been provided in Brent; they are now protected from encroachment, the largest being at Lower Place, behind Central Middlesex Hospital, acquired as part of the original infirmary site. The Kensal Rise Allotment Holders Association was founded about 1910 and continued its annual shows for many years thereafter. To the north, the Gladstone Park Horticultural Society ran successfully in a similar vein, although it started in the 1920s. It invited the veteran Lt. Col. Sir Charles Pinkham to its eighth annual show in 1932.

Plays and Games

Abortive theatre projects were proposed for Craven Park, Acton Lane (where later Willesden Crown Court was erected) and at the corner of Harlesden High Street and Furness Road.

112. *(Left)* Willesden Hippodrome, *c*.1920. It was destroyed during the Second World War.

113. *(Below)* Harlesden Philharmonic in 1937, later the Willesden Philharmonic and now the Brent Symphony Orchestra.

Willesden's only permanent theatre, the Hippodrome, had a shorter life than many of its compeers in the music-hall world. It opened on 16 September 1907 and was bombed in October 1940, never to re-open. It was on the circuit for all the great stars in the 40-year period of its activity. Its opening night, under the management of Percy Gallagher, included Prince de Broglie conducting the orchestra while the Princess sang; at the top of the bill was Alec Hurley, the husband of Marie Lloyd who herself appeared at the theatre later as did Vesta Tilley, G. H. Elliot (who, for a period lived in Willesden), George Robey and many others. It was bought by the young Sidney Bernstein in 1927 who renovated it and gave it a new lease of life for its remaining dozen years. Ernie Lotinga made one of his 'farewell' appearances here in 1928.

Arthur Lucan and his wife, Kitty McShane, who created the characters of Old Mother Riley and her daughter were very popular music-hall artistes of the 1930s and '40s. They lived for a period at 11 Forty Lane (Wembley), remembered by one of the G.L.C. blue plaques.

Amateur dramatic societies flourished particularly in the heyday of the non-professional groups in suburbia between the wars (and after the Second World War). Few have survived.

The Brent Symphony Orchestra started off in 1912 as the Harlesden Philharmonic Society, became the Willesden Symphony Orchestra and then acquired its present name to indicate its allegiance to the wider realm of the new borough. Harry Legge has been its conductor for many years, helping to extend its repertoire and its influence throughout the musical world in Brent.

In the 1920s, the Willesden Amateur Operatic Society and the Court Operatic Society both flourished. Bon Accord Operatic Society was formed in 1923 by Reginald Howe and his wife, Mabel Aitken who, in 1979, was still closely associated with the company. At that time it comprised, in the main, teachers and musicians from Willesden and has performed at halls in the borough and in London.

Sport Across the Years

The social and sporting life of the local communities sprang up to offer residents the chance to meet together and enjoy themselves. The Kilburn Cricket Club dates from the 1870s; the Kilburn and Maida Vale Poultry, Pigeon and Cage Bird Society from 1893; the College Park Musical Society, the St George's Literary Society at Willesden Green and the Willesden Hockey club were all flourishing in the 1890s. In 1885, a group of boys from Droop Street school, Queen's Park, Paddington, joined St Jude's Institute Football Club. They played on many pitches in Kensal Rise, Brondesbury and at Harvist Road where, acquiring the new name of Queen's Park Rangers in 1897, they began a wobbly but ultimately successful rise to fame.

These notes can only touch on a few of the hundreds of sporting clubs and societies formed in Willesden in the last hundred years or so.

Cricket: Before the First World War there was a cricket ground between Haycroft Farm and Roundwood House, roughly where Cardinal Hinsley school is today. However, the main cricket location in Willesden is the South Hampstead Club, despite its name. In 1875 a team called Crescent Cricket Club was playing in Regents Park, changing its name to South Hampstead in 1893 when it moved to a ground at Primrose Hill for a few years. Then, in 1900, the Club leased its present ground in Sidmouth Road. (After 60 years as tenants of the Church Commissioners, they were able to buy the freehold.) Milverton Road was still only fields at that time and the only houses in sight were a few large ones in Brondesbury Park including Brondesbury Manor House. As is often found in Club activities, families contributed much to success, and the names Brooman, Sherwell and Malcolm are among those honoured by South Hampstead. An old pavilion gave way in 1967 to a modern building of attractive design under the trees. An association with the Old Uffingtonians (Willesden County school) proved fruitful to both Clubs and recruits from other local schools were fostered.

Rugby clubs abounded as did Soccer; one can do scant justice to the thousands of players (and spectators) who over the years made these games an integral part of their weekly lives.

Angling was a long favoured sport—one of the most wide-spread of all, Harlesden Angling Society, can stand for all the others.

Swimming: Open-air pools were provided by Willesden in Gladstone Park in 1903 and King Edward's Recreation Ground in 1911. Another pool, sited in a corner of spare land at Craven Park, had only a short life from 1938 until it was destroyed during the Second World War and never re-opened. The Granville Road indoor baths, opened in 1937, were regarded at the time as a model of design and fitness for purpose. The pool at King Edward's became an indoor bath as part of the Willesden Sports Centre in 1966.

Willesden Swimming Club, although planned before the First World War, was founded at a

114. *(Left)* The open-air swimming pool in Gladstone Park, *c.*1905.

115. *(Below)* Granville Road baths shown here in 1937.

Volunteer was named and also Victoria Road. Another was off what is now Longstone Avenue, running from a point inside what later became Willesden cemetery into the knoll at Roundwood Park. Neasden Rifle Club operated in the years before the First World War, another was operated by Holland and Holland off the Harrow Road at the beginning of this century on the site that became the Kensal Rise Ground. The Rifle Volunteer movement used the drill hall in Pound Lane for many years, starting in 1911.

Other Sporting Activities: From about 1870 to 1910 a 'National Athletic Ground' was established at Kensal Rise. Queen's Park Harriers, a one-time celebrated local Athletic Club started in 1887 in Ilbert Street (on the Paddington estate) and among many other venues—they had a history of being chased out by the developers time after time— used the Kensal Rise Ground. Queen's Park Rangers played there occasionally and so did Kilburn Grammar School.

Golf was played in Willesden at Neasden, behind Neasden House (Links Road), there was a successful golf course for a period before and after the First World War. Part of the house served as a club house; part of the grounds, after the house had been pulled down, was used for St Catherine's church. The club proudly claimed Prince Arthur of Connaught as its President, just before 1914.

meeting at Pound Lane School in September 1919 under the chairmanship of Colonel Charles Pinkham. The Olympic Games in London in 1948 provided a welcome fillip to the Club who contributed two members to the British Swimming Team (Vera Ellery and Kathleen Cuthbert). Over the next few decades the Club produced other swimmers of international status.

Shooting: Shooting ranges and butts in the 19th century were at the Victoria Rifles' ground off Kilburn High Road from which the pub the *Rifle*

The Silver Screen
Although the cinema had its heyday in the inter-war period, it had an exciting build-up and, despite many counter-attractions, is by no means finished as a prime source of entertainment. One of the first organised film shows in our district seems to have been given at the Constitutional Hall in St Mary's Road in April 1902. Cinematograph

pictures of the Prince and Princess of Wales' cruise (later to become King George V), of the Japanese Navy and of the Royal Navy were shown to large 'houses' for five nights a week. These were described as 'a fine exhibition of the latest scientific development of photography'.

The first cinema giving regular performances was set up, again at the Constitutional Hall, by David Jamilly (born in 1880 in Singapore, died in London in 1949) and Percy Gallagher (late of the Willesden Hippodrome). They advertised in the *Willesden Chronicle* in October 1908 that animated pictures would be shown twice nightly at 6.50 and 9.0 pm. It was soon being called 'The Premier Electric Theatre'. The advertisement went on to say 'an entertainment that holds everybody. Plenty to laugh at. Nothing to shock you [that soon changed!]. 2 hours solid entertainment' and so on. The front row seats cost 1s., back 3d.—it was not then appreciated that being too close was not the best place to view moving pictures. Jamilly had to convince the customers that the cinema was respectable and so used to stand outside dressed in a frock coat.

Another early cinema was in a building adjacent to the *Coach and Horses* at Stonebridge. It had opened in 1908 as a Palace of Varieties, run by Jumbo Ecclestone (It is now the Caterers' Mart). In 1910 they even tried out a form of 'talking' using an instrument called a 'Vivaphone' said to be able to provide 'speaking and singing as perfectly as though it was the substance instead of the shadow'. However, just in case of difficulties, there was also the familiar silent-picture pianist.

Other early cinemas included the Little Palace in Cricklewood (1909), possibly next door to the Skating Rink (now the Galtymore); one at 192 Church Road and another at 103 Harlesden High Street, known as the People's Picture Palace.

In November 1911, the Picture House was opened at 24 Harlesden High Street (in the late 1920s it became Sanders the corn merchant—not so great a change as it might seem!), near the then offices of the Gas Light and Coke Company. It was run by a Mr. Polkinham (or Blinkhorn—one version of the name is given in a newspaper article, the other in an advertisement). At 120 Harlesden High Street yet another was opened just before Christmas 1911 by Sir William Treloar, patron of a fund for cripples (the only connection was to demonstrate, again, the respectability of the new entertainment). Its manager was Mr. N. Briggs and it was at first called the Harlesden and later the Picardy; eventually, after the Second World War, it became a dance-hall.

In August 1912 Omnium Electric Palaces Ltd (what glorious names they had in those days) opened the Rutland Park Cinema at 67-69 High Road, near the Willesden Green library. It could hold 500 people and cost one shilling for a reserved seat. There was a great ceremony as guests visited the cinema for the first time and viewed not only the auditorium but also the lounges and tea garden. Performances ran continuously from 3 to 11 p.m. every day except Sunday. However, in the early 1920s it became a 'Salon de Danse' and then a temperance billiard hall. Later it fell derelict and was pulled down to make an access to the Gateway food store.

Sunday cinema opening was the subject of much local controversy. It was debated in the Willesden council in 1914 and many times thereafter until 1933 when a town poll voted in favour.

By the end of the First World War the cinemas which were advertising in the local papers were: the Coliseum at Harlesden showing *The Garden of Allah* and including among its attractions the Coliseum Orchestra; there was the Rutland Park Cinema; the Pavilion at Kensal Rise (1916); the Kilburn Grange (1914), on the Hampstead side of Kilburn High Road but very popular with Willesden residents (and where I saw my first film—*Evergreen*). From its opening until the building of the State Cinema it was the largest cinema in the United Kingdom.

There was also the Picture Palace at Kensal Rise (1913) and the Maida Vale Picture House, a building of glorious Hollywood 'baroqueness' on the Hampstead side of the road (1912). Very popular was the Electric Palace, later called the Savoy at Chapel End (later still the Metro, then used for a variety of business uses) and the Electric Theatre in Lonsdale Road, Kilburn.

During the 1930s, there was a boom in the cinema. The Empire (later the Granada) at Church End (1929) was slightly ahead of its time—a typical venture of the young Sidney (later Lord) Bernstein—who had also acquired the Willesden Hippodrome. Odeons began to grace the scene, the product of the competitive genius of Oscar Deutsch. They were grand palaces in Art Deco style, havens for the weary, dark caverns of illuminated bliss. One of these was built at Harlesden (amid local protests).

The greatest of them all was—and still is, despite the changes—the Gaumont State at Kilburn. Built in 'neo-Renaissance' style to house 4,004 patrons it was, at first, announced as the largest cinema in the world, but Los Angeles went one better, so it became 'the largest cinema in Europe'. On 20 December 1937, a lavish opening ceremony with Gracie Fields (then at the height of her popularity) as principal guest was attended by a full house and a crush of onlookers, in

116.   The Coliseum in Manor Park Road, Harlesden in 1908.

117.   The Gaumont State cinema opened in 1937. A picture of decline.

118.   One of the earlier picture palaces, this was situated in Willesden Green High Road near Pound Lane. The illustration dates from 1917. The cinema was later called the Savoy and then the Metro.

Hollywood premiere style, in the High Road. The music was provided by Henry Hall and his Band, Van Dam and the State Broadcasting Orchestra and there was Larry Adler, George Formby and others on the opening bill.

The onset of war halted the cinema building boom. The 'big four'—Odeon (taken over by Rank when Deutsch died), ABC, Granada and Gaumont, all had their cinemas in Willesden. After the war, cinema-going continued its popularity until about 1950, when began the decline which has perhaps only recently been halted. While mainly brought about by the increasing presence of television, it was also due to changes in leisure habits and through greater mobility as car ownership spread.

Closures proceeded apace so that by about 1980 there was not one cinema left in the whole of Willesden (or, for that matter in Brent). The Electric Palace at Rockhall Terrace on the Hendon side of Cricklewood Broadway was demolished; the Ritz at Neasden went—to become a new branch library. The Granada at Church End was turned into the new craze—a bingo hall. The Picardy in Harlesden flourished for a while first as an Irish and then a Caribbean Social Club. Kensal Rise lost both its cinemas, one to a garage, the other to bingo. The Queen's in Cricklewood Lane gave way to shops and the Grange at Kilburn was converted into a large entertainment centre. There was an attempt to reopen the Harlesden Odeon (last cinema to be built in Willesden) as a theatre, the Roxy, but this had a short life—it was demolished to provide housing. One cinema restarted—a small one inside the once-great Gaumont State—but soon gave up. In 1992, a cinema was opened inside the new Willesden Green Library Centre.

Just for the record, a new 'cinema', the Bijou, was created in 1956 when a cardboard replica of a picture palace frontage was placed over a shop front in the High Road near Kilburn (Bakerloo) station. It was part of the scenery for the film *The Smallest Show On Earth*.

Pictures in the Making

There were several breath-taking occasions when Willesden (and then Wembley) were each on the edge of becoming a national film-production centre. From 1918 to 1926, Pearson-Elder made a number of films in what was then the third largest studio in Britain. This was at 41 Craven Park—previously a private grammar school and more recently the Willesden County Court (now demolished—yet another loss of our historical heritage).

In 1921, Sir Oswald Stoll formed a company for picture production using studios in Temple Road, Cricklewood. It was, as described in the press, 'a hive of industry'. It could happen that five films were being made at the same time. Edison films had studios for a while at 300 Victoria Road (just outside the area, to the south of Willesden Junction).

One footnote—in recent years, streets in Brent, schools and public buildings have been widely used as locations for films, television plays and commercial advertisements. The council encourage such exciting intrusions, reaping some modest income in the process.

Chapter 17

Satanic Mills and Devilish War

Industry Moves In

Saxby and Farmer, a railway signal engineering firm, was founded in the 1870s. By 1912 the site in Canterbury Road was used by the Humber motor car company and later by Raymond Way who built up a highly successful car sales organisation.

By about 1900 a few small firms in Kilburn, a foundry at Stonebridge, a biscuit works at Park Royal, laundries (including the White Heather) and small repair works in various parts of Willesden (Lonsdale Road was a particular centre) comprised the industrial scene.

By 1914 printing had established itself in Willesden as a local industry; light engineering firms, mostly small family businesses, were beginning to contribute to Willesden's image as a manufacturing area. Often they were in backyards or converted stables—'non-conforming' industry. Among the pre-First World War firms in the area were Dallmeyer optical lens manufacturers, Naris makers of table waters, Addressograph, NSU motors, Peradon billiard requisite manufacturers,

Crossley wire mattress makers, Cartona baking powder, Grant Legros type-casting machine makers, British-Thompson-Houston and a number of firms associated with car and cycle repairs, accessories and engineering, many of whom were in the Lonsdale and Salusbury road areas.

John Wooler started to build two-stroke motorcycles in Willesden in 1911. He soon had to expand and moved his works to the Ealing Road where the 'Flying Banana' was made—a well-known cycle at the time. It was streamlined, years ahead of its period, which helped its racing at Brooklands.

The extension of the railways through Park Royal and Alperton in the early 1900s helped to open up those areas to industrial development. After the First World War, the building of successive stretches of the North Circular Road was a powerful force for attracting firms to the adjacent land.

McVitie and Price was the biscuit factory mentioned earlier. Their Edinburgh Biscuit works

119. The Royal Willesden Laundry in the High Road, c.1912.

120. The Heinz factory was built in 1925.

was opened on a 12½- acre site in Waxlow Road. By this means they fostered the growing London trade in biscuits which, until then, had been supplied from Edinburgh itself. The factory boomed, soon employing 500 workers and producing a greater output than its parent. Much later it became part of the United Biscuits Group.

H. J. Heinz had founded his bottling and canning business in Pittsburgh, U.S.A. in 1869. To help capture a part of the expanding British market, a modern factory was erected in Waxlow Road in 1925. It now (1994) employs about 500 people who help to make some of the famed 57 varieties.

Wartime: The First World War

Fragments of wartime recollections are found in many publications of the war years and the post-war decades; a few of these will provide a picture of the patriotic fervour which pervaded the First World War period.

Some of the buses from Cricklewood garage were requisitioned, the drivers put in khaki uniform and used to transport troops to France. A flying field was established in Claremont Road, on the Hendon side of the Edgware Road, and became Handley Page's factory and testing ground.

'Kilburn VC Hero' was the local headline in October 1914 for Battery Sergeant Major George Dorrell of Kilburn Park Road. With two other members of his battery he won the award at the battle of Mons for—I can describe it no better way—'sticking to his guns'.

Firms switched their normal production to munitions. Many Willesden companies were involved in making aircraft parts, serving the industry which was now centred on Hendon and Kingsbury. Smiths clocks were just one firm heavily into the war effort.

At Dollis Hill there was a tank testing ground and the high wall which marked it off can still be seen at Tankridge Close.

Belgian refugees arrived in the autumn of 1914 in the wake of the invasion of their country, 'plucky Belgium', from their King and Queen to thousands of working class people. They were found lodgings all over Britain, Willesden taking a share. A soirée was held by the Willesden Committee for Refugees at Salusbury Road School on 2 January 1915, under its President George Hiscock.

Normality was often the theme—yes, war was terrible, but life went on. Kilburn Grammar School staged its play night; cinemas continued to show their films, including the 'new' Grange on the Hampstead side of the Kilburn High Road; musical societies, garden and allotment associations held their shows, though vegetables were more on display, to help the war effort. Often they used their efforts to support war charities. War Savings schemes competed for ways to serve the cause, and food rationing was bravely, if glumly, accepted—Frank Chennell the borough librarian taking on the thankless task of organising the local arrangements—and also the scheme for conscription. Not forgotten were the needs of the soldiers at the Front—there as an appeal for boots from a driver in the Royal Field Artillery. Men queued to join up, especially after the intimidating 'white feather' campaign. It was still not enough; women joined the women's civil corps and struck a resounding blow for women's rights and votes.

Sadly enough, lists of local men who were killed, or missing, were a regular feature of the local newspapers. Thankfully, though, unlike the Second World War, civilian air raid casualties were few. A few bombs dropped by a Gotha aircraft fell on or near Belsize Road on 28 January 1918 and one in Oxford Road and one on the railway sidings in Canterbury Road on 19 May 1918, in the last raid on London. There was little damage. One open-top tram was converted to carry a searchlight on its upper deck and travelled up and down the Edgware Road from Canons Park.

One of the largest local changes involved the care for the sick and wounded. Dollis Hill House became a war hospital. Places like St Matthew's Hall and houses in Brondesbury Park and elsewhere added to the facilities of Willesden Cottage and St Andrew's Hospitals.

Astonishingly perhaps for 1916, a Maternity and Child Welfare Centre was set up in Willesden Lane. School meals by the thousand were provided to ensure that children, at least, had adequate nourishment. A day and night nursery for children of munitions workers was set up at Park Royal.

The *Willesden Chronicle* recorded in its last issue of 1918: 'The war ended, alas, with many gallant men lost to us for ever, except in deathless memories of their successful struggle for our freedom, recorded on many war memorials and shrines. Thanksgiving services for peace and the visit of the King and Queen after the armistice to their rejoicing local subjects have fittingly closed these terrible war years.'

Chapter 18

Aftermath of War

Homes for Heroes

Willesden was one of the first authorities in the country to accede to the government's post-war plea for houses (Lloyd George's 'Homes for Heroes') to make up for the war-time shortage. Twyford and Stonebridge were both considered but the former site was thought to be unsuitable. Sixty-three acres at Stonebridge were started in 1920, commencing with the Dog Lane site at Wright's Farm, near the sewage farm (the original St Raphael's Estate). The North Circular Road was planned but not yet built; it formed the eastern boundary of this site and split it from the rest of the development nearer to the *Coach and Horses*. About 570 houses and 42 flats were built. The Ministry of Health recommendations for housing to Tudor Walters' standards were used.

The Estate roads were mostly given field names—Normansmead (a farm holding), Brentfield Close, Pitfield Way, Dryfield Close and Foxholt Gardens (after 'foxholes'). Wyborne Way was named after another farm holder, Twybridge Way because of the two bridges over the canal feeder (also an echo of Twyford) and Durand Way after the Domesday Book Canon. A small corner of the estate near the *Coach and Horses* was actually within the Wembley parish, but although agreement was nearly reached between the two councils in 1926 to transfer the land to Willesden, it had to wait until 1933 before the exchange actually took place.

Cunning and unscrupulous opponents of slum clearance, as the mayor of Willesden called them in 1933, seized on the vagueness of the terms in the 1930 Housing Act to delay the good intentions of progressive boroughs. This act was put forward by the Labour Housing Minister, Arthur Greenwood and it proved to be another milestone in housing legislation.

The mayor of Willesden also said, in October 1933, 'The Clearance of Slum areas received a great amount of publicity, nationally and locally, and whilst we may perhaps count ourselves lucky in not possessing any well defined "slums" there are still large areas that must receive the attention of the Willesden programme.'

One of the first fruits of this zeal by the new Borough was the building of the housing estate at Curzon Crescent, to rehouse people from the slums of Kilburn. The estate was named after the statesman, Lord Curzon (1859-1925), also a Fellow of All Souls. The estate, then known as 'Church End', was built in 1935-36. It included, in its first stage, 206 flats costing £99, 679 to build and 60 houses at £22, 475, with roads and sewers another £7,881. Former Councillor Mrs. Vi Wallis described to me the 'accident' which set fire to the empty, lousy and verminous slums, Alpha Place, Kilburn, making sure they could never again be used for housing. Nonetheless, some people refused at first to move because of higher rents and took a lot of persuading.

A nursery school was built at the entrance to the estate which proved to be an attraction to many visitors who were interested in the open air situation and freedom from overly strict controls.

The Private Builders

We now take 'suburbia' and Metroland for granted. The Grange Museum has a section illustrating a typical 1930s house interior.

In Willesden, private builders helped create the 'semi-detached' suburb. An outstanding example was off Anson Road, where the All Souls' Estate was extended with the building of four-bedroomed houses, brick-built integral garages and all labour-saving devices. This second or even third wave of building on College land led to further ransacking of the All Souls' records for suitable names. Sneyd, Gardiner, James (Wardens), Oman (historian), Dicey (a famous jurist) and Wren—the famous architect who designed All Souls' College.

The relentless tide of bricks and concrete could not be stayed. The rural hinterland of Gladstone Park at the top of Dollis Hill included Neasden House (which became flats known as Neasden

121. Neasden: the local shopping centre in the 1930s.

122. Dewsbury Road, *c.*1910. The scene depicted is typical of early suburbia; the vista remains but now tree-lined.

Court before its eventual demolition). Its grounds became the quickly-devoured victims of the 1930s boom in building as Britain rose out of the great depression. When I was at primary school in Willesden, at this period, one of my classmates, who lived at a farm on the Hill, was driven to lessons in a pony and trap. Neasden shopping centre, with the Ritz Cinema, grew up to serve this large neighbourhood.

The build-up of the north-west suburbs of London along the line of the Metropolitan Railway outwards from Willesden Green to the Chilterns was given the name 'Metroland' by an enterprising publicist. A hint of its pre-war glamour is exquisitely expressed in some of Sir John Betjeman's poems. It was largely the result of a house building expansion carried out directly by or inspired by the estates development offshoot of the Metropolitan Railway Company.

It was responsible, after the First World War, for the Kingsbury Garden Village—an extension westwards of the original estate for railway workmen at Quainton Street. Other developments were at Sherrick Green near Gladstone Park where the road names had been started before the First World War and were continued in ABC style: Aberdeen, Burnley, Cullingworth, Dewsbury, Ellesmere ... Hamilton ... Lancaster.

In the late 1930s, I saw Brondesbury Manor House (which had become a girls' boarding school) and its Park, for the last time. Willesden council hoped to buy the estate for the new civic centre but were outbid by developers who then built a fashionable estate of high-class houses, including Manor House Drive.

Between 1919 and March 1940, Willesden built 1,815 houses and, in addition, private developers, using subsidies provided under the Housing Act, built 948. However, private developers without recourse to public funds built over 9,400 houses in Willesden.

Road and Rail
The North Circular Road was devised during the First World War. It was originally named in Willesden, between Neasden and the Harrow Road, 'North Way'. In the building of the new road, the central section of Dog Lane, crossing the Metropolitan Railway near Neasden station, disappeared. It left a short stretch near the *Old Spotted Dog* under its original name. The southern section, passing Neasden Hospital, was renamed Brentfield Road. The North Circular Road in Willesden was completed in 1934. It continued to Hanger Lane in Ealing. The viaduct carrying the canal over it was built without interrupting the traffic. The IRA tried to blow it up in 1939.

Parliamentary action to prevent 'ribbon building' on the new major trunk and arterial roads came too late in 1935. In Willesden, the local council was the main offender and built its estates on both sides of and right up to the North Circular Road. This has resulted in a perpetual, unrelenting, unwinnable war against traffic noise by the hapless residents.

The bus network as a whole was little different from that of today—it was the frequency that was much greater in those days in response to the needs of a largely car-less society. Tram services began to be converted, more or less unchanged in route, to trolley buses in 1936-37. The tramlines, long a danger to cyclists, were removed and the old wood road blocks went for fuel.

In the 1920s, private bus operators—'pirates'—were rife. The immediate post-war period saw a steep rise in unemployment. Some ex-soldiers bought ex-army buses to make a living for themselves. Some were employed by the LGOC but then made redundant. One was Joe Ryan of Sandringham Road in Willesden Green who ran a 218E2 service from King's Cross to Sudbury. The Stevens Brothers of Westbury Road, Church End, ran the Pioneer services.

The London Traffic Act (1924) permitted a degree of controlled competition with the hitherto monopoly of the LGOC. The biggest threat came from the Birch Brothers whose family had started in the coaching business in 1832—the brothers came into being in 1899. The 231 ran on the route between Hampstead Heath and Willesden Junction, based on a unique agreement with the LGOC. With the introduction of London Transport in 1933, all independent operators had to cease and some routes, like Birch Bros., were absorbed into the public network.

The extension of the Tube into the suburbs and the development of outer suburban London are instances of the chicken and egg situation—which came first: houses or railways? Metropolitan Railways built the Stanmore extension through the new Kingsbury development in 1930 to 1932. It was one of the speediest train constructions ever. With the new Labour government in 1929 intent on reducing unemployment, financial aid was made available. By late 1930 the whole approval process was under way. The line was later transferred to the Bakerloo line and then to the Jubilee.

Chapter 19

Getting Industry Moving

Industry Expands

In 1923, the *Estates Gazette* reported: 'The extraordinary growth of Willesden Green and Harlesden and the likelihood of new suburbs and commercial prosperity continually expanding generally inspires investors to favour these districts'. The development of the new arterial roads like Western Avenue and the North Circular Road did much to stimulate this post-war enthusiasm. Willesden had a strong concentration of general engineering (right up until the mid-1960s) and a great variety of industries grew up. They were drawn by a number of factors: the availability of labour close at hand; good rail and canal communications; the opportunity for a healthier, cleaner environment; and close proximity to the West End of London.

By 1933, a survey revealed a ten-fold growth in factories in the previous 20 years. Between the 1930s and the 1960s, the area of Park Royal and Perivale (with the adjacent parts of Wembley and Willesden) was regarded as the greatest single concentration of manufacturing industry in southern England. There were 70 factories on the Park Royal Estate, just across the border and 30 in various parts of Willesden with about 10,000

123.   Waterlow's printing the *Radio Times* in the 1920s, in Park Royal.

124. Heinz workers, *c*.1930.

people working in them. The variety of goods manufactured in these factories is a compendium of British industry: pencils and pens, boots and shoes, spring mattresses, wireless sets, dynamos, metals and machinery, gramophones, patent foods such as Virol, Spearmint and Carltona custard, chemical products, motor equipment, paper products, lenses and dozens of others.

Smith's Industries came to the Edgware Road during the First World War. Samuel Smith was a Victorian watchmaker who built up a firm which exploited this skill by making time recorders and then, as the motor age dawned, automobile equipment such as speedometers. Wartime needs led to further expansion and works were built at Temple Road, Cricklewood where another new invention—the aeroplane—demanded specialised instruments. After the war, in the 1920s, the firm turned to electric clocks as one development and, as another, to even more sophisticated aircraft instrumentation such as the Smith's Flight System used in many modern aircraft. Further expansion of its technical skills caused the firm to acquire more premises so that there were, at its peak, Smith's factories dotted all over Cricklewood.

This firm should not be confused with Smith's Potato Crisps. Frank Smith started crisp production in a garage in Cricklewood in 1919. Then as success beckoned, he moved to a factory on the North Circular Road. By the mid-1950s the firm had 80 per cent of the market, provided from factories all over Britain. Later still, the forces of competition drove them out of Willesden, though still active elsewhere.

The empty acres alongside the main roads beckoned to the eager manufacturers looking for premises so as to benefit from the post-First World War boom.

Not only were houses built right on to the North Circular Road but so were factories in North Cricklewood. This is not to criticise the firms which needed to expand and who went where land was available. Particularly unfortunate was the development of land between the north side of the North Circular Road and the Welsh Harp in a way which despoils the aspect of the open space around the reservoir.

In 1926 on the south side, at the junction with Edgware Road, Harold Heal opened his factory for the production of Staples mattresses and this

125. Smith's Electric in Cricklewood during the 1960s.

126. Staples' Corner—the firm gave its name to the building which is now demolished but the name lingers on. This photograph dates from 1926.

added a new name to the *London Gazeteer*—Staples' Corner. Even before the First World War, Heals had been enquiring about sites for expansion—one of these letters came to Willesden. It was not until Colonel Pinkham's North Circular Road was built that fields belonging to Upper Oxgate Farm were seen to be the best location and were promptly acquired. Built to the design of P. M. Fraser, the combination of a single-storey works with a two-storey office block with enamelled iron plates carrying the name of the firm and its products, produced a building often referred to as typical of its period. Its distinctive landmark was overshadowed by the two-level junction complex and, sadly, it has since been demolished.

Nearby along the North Circular Road towards Neasden during the next ten years came factories for lamps, die-casting, biscuits, general and electrical engineering, cinema equipment, chocolate, glass (Tobias), oxygen (British Oxygen), plate glass and welding. The National Cash Register Company came in but left in 1978. The attraction of the area was partly in the communications afforded by the comparatively new North Circular Road and partly the cheap and plentiful supply of electricity from Willesden's undertaking which served nearly 40,000 installations. (In 1935, 64.5 million electricity units were sold including 3 million for street lighting.) Along the Edgware Road, Remploy, the post-war creation of the Welfare State to help disabled

127. Industry on the North Circular Road. Meltonian illuminated for the Silver Jubilee in 1935.

people into employment, founded its main factory and Head Office.

Skilled labour and, even more, unskilled labour, was being demanded at a rate Willesden could not meet. People travelled daily from other parts of London or crowded into the area to live, two or three families inhabiting what had been built as suburban villas for city workers 20 or 30 years earlier (see *Willesden Survey* 1949).

On a small scale this had been the situation in Kilburn Park in the 1870s; it was repeated throughout our history. In Kilburn alone, in the 1930s, there were more industrial concerns than there had been in the whole of Willesden in 1910 although these were mostly small scale in Lonsdale Road and nearby. North Cricklewood was establishing itself as an industrial zone and so was Church End. Many small industrial firms were established among residential property. In 1935, Willesden was able to claim that it was one of the most important industrial centres around London; many of the factories modern and up-to-date. Yet, by 1965 there was considerable anxiety over the run-down of industry in the Brent area, particularly Willesden and Park Royal, with the consequent loss of jobs.

In addition, the range of industrial activity and products manufactured was a justification of the claim made about the importance of Willesden. From acetylene welding to zinc working, the list included cabinet making and joinery, engineering in manifold varieties and the production of blinds, boxes, furniture, perfumes, scientific instruments, stationery, table waters, tents, transformers and much else.

The hunger marchers from the depressed North and Wales made for London. In 1934, one of these marches was to be greeted by the 'Willesden Hunger March Solidarity Committee' who tried, apparently unsuccessfully, to obtain overnight accommodation for the 350 marchers. The Committee's meetings were carefully kept under surveillance by the police.

The biggest factory of all, and certainly the most attractive, was—and is—that of Guinness. In 1934 the national newspapers carried reports of a mystery million-pound factory being built on a 120-acre site at Park Royal on the former Royal Agricultural Show ground. It was said to be for making alcohol from potatoes ('which could provide Britain with a home supply of fuel for motorcars and aeroplanes'). Within a few weeks the mystery was revealed—the building was to be Guinness's English brewery. It was designed by Sir Giles Gilbert Scott, as notable an architect as his grandfather whose early work included St John's church, Wembley. A bold brick building, it is in similar style to the Battersea power station and is a notable addition to the architecture of the 1930s. A model village for workers was to be built as part of the scheme, with a cinema, shops and a school.

The foundations of the brewery went deep into the ground and the steel superstructure rose over one hundred feet in the air. An artesian well was bored to obtain water which was reported to be of practically the same quality as that used in Dublin. It was this factor which dictated the choice of site. In 1936 the first brew was made—thereafter it supplied the whole of Southern England.

The first houses on the Guinness estate were not built until 1947 at Moyne Place (mostly in the borough of Ealing). It was one of a number of street names associated with the family—including Elveden Place (after their seat in Norfolk) and Iveagh Avenue (the title assumed by the fourth Chairman, Edward Cecil Guinness 1847-1927). A primary school was built by Ealing council at West Twyford in 1940.

Local residents sought to turn the proposed new estate to their advantage by asking for a station on the nearby railway. London Transport said that as Park Royal and Alperton stations were only a mile apart they could not agree.

In 1976 Guinness paid about half-a-million pounds in rates to Brent out of a sales income of £82 million, half of which is beer duty. They then employed about 1,500 staff. Their contribution to the community is widespread and generous, including Brent's civic regalia.

The Glacier Metal Company was formed in 1899 by two Americans, C. W. Findley and A. S. Battle, to manufacture and market anti-friction alloys. The manufacture of bearings was carried out at first at a small factory in Waldo Road, College Park, just across the boundary from Willesden Junction. The First World War gave impetus to the use of the internal combustion engine and increased the demand for plain bearings. In December 1923, the works moved to Alperton, next to the 'cottage' occupied by Wooler Cycles.

In the heart of Willesden, at Church End, the prestigious firm of Rolls Royce acquired the old-established body-building company of Park Ward and later that of H. J. Mulliner (on the site of Woodbine Cottages and an old farm-house which was used as offices), merging the two in 1959 and moving to the High Road in 1961. Just across the southern border, in Hythe Road, Rolls Royce had operated their own car servicing premises from 1938.

In Dudden Hill Lane in 1928, F. W. Hall established his factory for manufacturing telephone coin boxes. This was Hall's Telephone Accessories (HTA). Hall, a prolific and fertile inventor, perfected the stamp-vending machine, still in use today, before turning to the machine on which his, and the firm's, reputation was founded. Later the company became known as Associated Automation. In the 1980s it closed, despite a valiant attempt by the workers to establish a co-operative to continue running it.

A few hundred yards away in Neasden Lane, British-Thomson-Houston (the British branch of an American subsidiary of General Electric Company of America) erected a large engineering works early in the 1920s. A few years later, BTH merged with Metropolitan-Vickers to form Associated Electrical Industries.

In 1967, the major series of mergers stimulated by the Labour government and the Industrial Reorganisation Corporation gave the British General Electric Company (under Arnold

128.   Work in progress on the Guinness factory in October 1934.

129. Hall's Phones, Dudden Hill Lane, repairing the famous coin boxes in the 1950s.

130. British-Thomson-Houston in Neasden Lane in the 1950s. It is now the site of Chancel House.

Weinstock) control of AEI and of English Electric. 'Rationalisation' was the favoured word; the AEI works in Neasden closed, making a major contribution to the run-down of Brent industries and throwing many men and women out of work. The site was redeveloped as offices (Chancel House) and as a new Magistrates' Court.

Following in the tradition of printing in Willesden, Oxford University Press built a warehouse in Neasden—the road is appropriately named Press Road. It opened in 1930 and was extended in 1961 and 1965 when a computer office block was opened by the late Sir Maurice Bowra, Warden of Wadham College, Oxford. (It closed in 1982 and the council bought the site for housing.)

The General Post Office opened their large research station on top of Dollis Hill in 1934 to carry out a wide range of experimental and development projects on communications. Its deep and cavernous basement rooms were used for occasional Cabinet meetings during the Second World War. Its dominant presence makes a landmark to be seen right across the Brent Valley. When the Post Office pulled out to a new site in East Anglia in the late 1970s, the buildings were taken over partly by the Willesden College of Technology, by Brent Social Services and by individual private firms.

At the start of the Second World War there were probably some 460 industrial firms in Willesden. This represented an absolute increase over the previous decade; in fact new firms came in at a rapid rate but older ones left the area or went out of business leaving a small net growth.

General Strike

> By breakfast time on Tuesday, 4th May 1926 between one and a half and two million workers were on strike. The largest strike in British history and the only one organised by the TUC had begun.
>
> (Margaret Morris, *The General Strike*, Penguin, 1976).

Over the whole of Willesden the response to the strike at factories, railway stations and depots and elsewhere was over 90 per cent, reaching nearly 100 per cent, according to an estimate by the Plebs League at the time.

Those who went to work travelled by all means of vehicles—carts, cars, bicycles—as public transport was at a standstill (although a 247 bus from Sudbury to King's Cross was actually operated and volunteers ran a 15-minute service on the Metropolitan line from Baker Street to Harrow). A local Council of Action was formed by the borough Labour Party in Willesden and all local trade union branches. The Labour Headquarters was set up at Hamilton Hall in the High Road, near Pound Lane (now the Trades and Labour Hall); meetings were held on Pound Green where some played football to while away the time.

Strikers also signed on at the memorial hall in Tubbs Road. A daily *Strike Bulletin* was published, giving news of nationwide strike activity as well as the local Willesden details.

Willesden council's electrical workers at first responded to an appeal from Labour councillors not to go on strike, because they were on essential work. However, this attitude changed in response to the TUC's call and they came out. Willesden council then called on volunteers and the service was resumed, although this decision was opposed by the Labour councillors. Non-unionists joined in the strike and unions like the Amalgamated Engineering Union made many new members, particularly from the 'worst firm in the district viz BTH'. (Letter from AEU Willesden Strike Committee to the TUC, 10 May 1926.)

Willesden council (not Labour controlled) decided to open four school halls with the use of piano for social and recreation meetings by the strikers. On 10 May the Education Committee, decided to feed the school children, beginning with 750 in necessitous areas.

It was reported by the strikers that 'we have found our best friends among the church people who have put premises (at schools and church halls) at our disposal'.

The strike was over in 10 days and, although the memory of it will remain forever, its effects in a place like Willesden, unlike in the mining villages, were soon over.

Chapter 20

Willesden Becomes a Borough

Willesden Proudly Gets its Charter

In 1931 Willesden was still the most populous district council in the county. It had long considered it was entitled to borough or even county-borough status. An Incorporation Committee was again established and the formal procedures under the Local Government Acts were started by a petition to the King-in-Council, followed, in 1932, by a thorough enquiry by a Ministry of Health Inspector.

The report of the Inspector recommending the granting of borough status was referred to the Privy Council and approval was duly given. The Incorporation Committee took on the role of Charter Celebration Committee as the preparations for the day of glory were put in hand.

An application was submitted to the College of Heralds for grant of armorial bearings for the new corporation. There was a souvenir brochure to be prepared—and very handsome it turned out to be.

With a subtle mixture of meanness and political craft, an appeal was launched for public contributions so that neither the festivities, the mace nor the mayoral regalia was paid for from the rates.

Prominent citizens and businessmen responded to the call. The Willesden Clerical Staff Association provided the mace while the mayoral badges and chains were supplied through the good offices of business houses led by McVitie and Price, and Heinz.

On 7 September 1933, Sir Percy Greenaway, genial Lord Mayor of London, was met at the borough boundary at Kilburn and taken in procession to the All Souls' Avenue entrance of the King Edward recreation ground where he presented the charter to the Mayor, Councillor Hiscock. Luncheon was taken at Wykeham School where a Charter Ball was held in the evening. To mark the occasion, a parcel of groceries was given to families of needy people.

131. Willesden Charter: 7 September 1933. The Lord Mayor of London was Guest of Honour.

It was not possible to provide a sit-down tea for all the children, so a tea box (with the borough arms painted on) was presented to each child in a council school together with a souvenir card. Best of all, they had a holiday from school—in the morning. For the next three days King Edward's park throbbed to the busy wheels of a fair.

When the elections for the new borough took place on 11 November 1933, Labour won control—which was never wrested from them during the lifetime of Willesden borough. Labour had 22 councillors and the moderates (i.e. Conservatives and allies) eleven.

Housing and health were the main aims of the new council and plans were made to cover the whole of Willesden with a number of health centres—but the war put an end to that dream. Public buildings were erected, such as Granville Road Baths and Electricity House in Willesden Lane, which were architecturally attractive in design and purposeful for their intended uses.

Health and Happiness?
At Hillside, Stonebridge, the Willesden health centre was inaugurated on 8 April 1930 by the Right Hon. Arthur Greenwood, Minister of Health in the second Labour government. Chairing the proceedings was W. A. Hill from Willesden district council and the 'top table' included a chairman of the Health Committee, William Bolton, Sir Charles Pinkham and Sam Viant, the local M.P.

It was one of the first such centres in England—the first in Willesden and specially designed for its purpose. It was intended to deal with every need of mother and child.

With the development of the health service a new, larger centre was built further up Hillside and in 1976 the clinic became an Adult Training Centre, still fulfilling a service to those in need.

At no.2 Buckingham Road, in the 1950s, was the practice of Dr. Hastings Banda, earlier known as 'the poor man's doctor'. He returned to Malawi (Nyasaland) in 1958 and, on independence in 1964, became Prime Minister and later Life President.

Health and Poverty
In 1875 the Medical Officer of Health on Willesden Local Board reported:

> Large numbers of newly-built houses, being let out in tenements and single rooms, attract a class of persons barely able to obtain necessaries of life, amongst these not a few are of intemperate and demoralised habits, with feeble vital stamina. Consequently there will be a larger proportion of chronic pauperism, sickness, and deaths. To this cause it is (as also to negligence and ignorance, and want of cleanliness and attention on the part of mothers to their offspring) that I attribute the excessive infant mortality. I find often too, that both parents go out to work, leaving their infants to the care of others (sometimes to older children).

The Middlesex County Medical Officer of Health said in 1933:

132. Young patients and their nurses, c.1905.

Study of the vital statistics for the County shows that the health of the people of Middlesex has been well sustained. The birth-rate was the highest since 1922, and the infantile mortality rate equal to that of 1929 which was the lowest on record. Although influenza was fairly prevalent towards the close of the year, epidemic illness has re-mained within reasonable limits and the inci-dence and mortality of diphtheria have set up new low records, due without any doubt to a vigorous policy of immunisation.

Improved housing seemed to be the answer to most of these problems. Overcrowding led to poor health. In 1952 the Willesden medical office of health reported that this problem created the difference between the three worst areas of Roundwood, Carlton and Stonebridge compared with Neasden. The present-day contrast between, say, Harlesden and Brondesbury Park would be even greater, despite the easing of some of the worst features of the post-war period.

The *Willesden Story* said of the 1950s:

Generations before, uncounted babies had died in Willesden as elsewhere, always the first to succumb to bad conditions. Willesden could proudly record that in 1955 the rate had fallen to a new low level only 20 dying of every thousand born. But still four babies died in Carlton for every one that died in Cricklewood; still the unfortunate parents who lost their babies were more often the unskilled and lower paid workers. Much was done for the mothers and babies through maternity and child welfare clinics.

Smoke and atmospheric pollution added to the lung congestion and self-mortification of the cigarette smoker. The medical superintendent of Central Middlesex Hospital said that the local power stations (at Taylors Lane and Acton Lane) were 'Appalling annexes to hell'. The Clean Air Act of 1956 began an improvement which has continued and has completely converted the borough into a smokeless territory.

The mentally afflicted, by illness or handicap, were identified and cared for in day centres, homes (which became less like institutions) and, increasingly, within the community. (It is a sad fact that one in 20 will spend some part of their life in a mental hospital.)

The first and last stages of Shakespeare's seven ages of man have attracted the compassionate attention of the county and borough councils. The number of day nurseries was expanded slowly and children's homes were provided.

Old people were provided for in many ways. For those who could fend for themselves there were flats with a resident warden like Lawnfield in Willesden.

Old people's centres, luncheon clubs and meals-on-wheels service were increasingly offered to the delighted senior citizens.

In Brent, in 1972, shortly before the service was transferred to the reconstructed health authority, the director of health commented favourably on services provided at health centres, about a free birth control service and of facilities provided to meet the emergency of an influx of refugees from Amin's Uganda.

The Board of Guardians and Central Middlesex Hospital

In October 1895, Frederick Priest, one of the Willesden members on the Hendon Union Board of Guardians, organised a successful campaign to separate Willesden from Hendon. The workhouse at Edgware was overcrowded; 250 of the 350 crowded inmates were from Willesden.

The Local Government Board speedily agreed with the proposal and in August 1896 Willesden became its own Poor Law District. Twenty-one Guardians were elected, three from each of the seven wards. J. A. Adams, a Middlesex county councillor (and a Conservative Party agent), was the first chairman. J. Hutton Haylor became clerk, at £200 a year, a post, among others, which he held until his death in 1938, aged 72.

Searching for a site for its workhouse infir-mary, the Board decided to purchase for £14,000 about 60 acres on the Twyford Abbey Estate at Acton Lane including Ruckholt, or Little Lower Place, Farm. The vendor was Colonel W. Doug-las-Willan, a descendant of the Thomas Willan who had built Twyford Abbey (also a relative of Lord Robert Boothby). The foundation stone was laid in April 1900 by the Willesden Board's chair-man with local dignitaries present; bands played; prayers were offered up; speeches were made. It was planned as six double-ward blocks of two storeys for 616 individuals but all that could be built with the funds available accommodated 150 sick people and 250 workhouse inmates (old and infirm). It opened in March 1903, the buildings still forming the central section of the present Central Middlesex Hospital.

The infirmary continued to act in its dual capacity through the First World War until 1930 when, after the MCC had the previous year taken over the administration of the Poor Law, Park Royal Hospital (as it had become) was handed

133. *(Left)* The Infirmary Board of Guardians, *c*.1900. On the right are Joseph and Elizabeth Brierley, the Workhouse master and matron. Second on the left, in the front row, is Miss M. H. Frost, matron of the Cottage Hospital. The Infirmary is now the Central Middlesex Hospital.

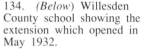

134. *(Below)* Willesden County school showing the extension which opened in May 1932.

over. The transfer included 24 acres of allotments which were leased to the Willesden council as the Lower Place allotment site. In 1931 the institution was renamed Central Middlesex Hospital and it so remained through the introduction of the National Health Service in 1948, up until the present time (1994), though now a Trust Hospital.

Schools

The only new secondary school to be built in the inter-war period was Willesden County Grammar.

Primary schools were also provided—Braintcroft and Wykeham to serve the families in the private and council estates on the slopes of Dollis Hill facing the Welsh Harp, as well as Infant and Junior schools to serve the area at Gladstone Park.

The Willesden Technical College was established in Denzil Road in 1934, a handsome building on a good site which was later to be heavily built over with extensions.

Education in Willesden was, for much of this period, dominated by the powerful figure of its Chief Education officer, Dr. Evan Davies—himself now recalled in the Nursery School at Stonebridge.

Education was compulsory only to age 14 and schools were organised here, as elsewhere, to cater for the majority who left as soon as they were legally able. For the minority, who wanted academic or technical education, there were the grammar and senior schools.

Under the 1902 Education Act Willesden ran its elementary schools virtually unimpeded by the county council, which was responsible for all other education.

Children celebrated Mayday and Empire Day, as well as the occasional Coronation. Playground games, before television dragged them indoors, were active and social—and educative. Whether the years up to the Second World War were a 'Golden Age' is for debate; children learned their essentials, but little else, other than the favoured few. It was part of a struggle for life which the later welfare state ameliorated and, I believe, helped to improve our chances.

Chapter 21

War Comes Again

The possibility of war's fiery dragons erupting over Britain twice in a life-time for many people began to haunt the more perceptive from 1936 onwards. References to Air Raid Precautions (ARP) began to appear in the reports of the Willesden council in 1938: 'Circulars and notes came from the Government 'in reams rather than in sheets' and almost everything had to give way to this new danger' (*The Willesden Story*).

Willesden schools debated the issues; trenches were dug in parks; council staffs adopted a second, war-shadowing role.

No one could foretell what war would really be like, but the preparations included 'Anderson shelters', gas-mask issue and provision of decontamination centres at the swimming baths and a decentralised civil defence scheme with local 'hubs' from which the essential services could operate. After the war, the hubs became youth centres—a sensible 'swords into ploughshares' operation.

Probably the most striking evidence of the imminence of war was the evacuation of mothers and children. To take one example, from personal experience, the carefully detailed and prepared plans suddenly became reality on Friday, 1 September 1939. Children and mothers (not always paired) made their way to the assigned station. For some of us from Willesden this was Kilburn High Road—the unfamiliar and rarely used platforms for the main line trains. We assembled, labelled and crowded together at the station, then joined a train for an 'unknown destination' which, in our case, turned out to be to the north of Northampton (though most soon gravitated to that town from the villages around). My mother, my very young sister and I were lodged (the *mot juste*) in the gatehouse of Creaton House, the home of the squire of the village. With wasps buzzing round the jam, we listened to the radio on the morning of Sunday, 3 September to hear Neville Chamberlain's sorrowful announcement that we were 'now at war with Germany'.

The first few months of the war were so quiet that, despite the blackout, separation and the shortages, it was called the 'phoney war'. In May 1940 'blitzkrieg' on the Western Front began; by 3 June, with Dunkirk behind them, the Germans were on the Channel coast. In August the battle of Britain began, launched against London and the south east by air bombardment. On 24 August, the first bomb fell on Willesden.

London was under full-scale attack until May 1941. Almost every day and night the air raid wardens, the fire service and the rescue teams were stretched, sometimes beyond endurance; so were the people. 'I can't bear it , I can't bear it! If them sirens go again tonight, I shall die'—the words of a 40-year-old Kilburn woman quoted from the Mass-Observation archives in 'Living through the Blitz'. It was a stringent test of the 'hub system' based at Gladstone Park, Roundwood

135. Second World War bomb damage in Clarence Road.

Park and Gibbons recreation ground. Yet we listened in the evenings to ITMA and Bandwagon, for laughter eases the pain that may come tomorrow.

Millions of pounds were saved in National Savings—to buy aircraft or war-ships or for comforts for the troops—over a million pounds in Willesden to one fund—'Wings for Victory'.

Willesden was not spared any of the ghastly array of war horrors—incendiary bombs, land mines, delayed action high-explosive bombs and, in the last year of the war, V1 'flying bombs' and V2 rockets. Everyone who lived through those years has some unforgettable memories of raids and incidents. The following extract from *The Willesden Story* is very compelling:

> When the shelters at the Technical College were bombed, ten people were killed and Willesden Civil Defence workers were recognised for their bravery in rescuing people. The eleven policemen who were killed when the bomb destroyed Salusbury Road Police Station; the injuries to every man and woman on duty at Stonebridge Fire Station when it was bombed; the ordinary citizens who were

injured and killed through the whole of Willesden's ordeal; the fire-fighters who had to cope with more than a hundred and forty fires on one night alone—all these incidents speak of a community who faced and fought a common danger together.

Through the difficult years, the factories and the work people continued to make their contribution to bringing the war to a victorious end.

Enemy raids on London resumed in January 1943 and continued until the savage blitzes early in 1944.

In 1944 Hitler's new 'secret' weapons, the flying bombs and rockets, were launched in a campaign to terrorise Britain and, almost immediately, a flying bomb struck near the boundary of Willesden and Acton, damaging houses in Willesden.

On five consecutive Wednesday nights, flying bombs fell on Willesden. One of the worst incidents was at College Road where, in bright daylight, a number of houses and some shops filled with customers were demolished; 20 people were killed and almost 100 injured. On Shoot-up-Hill one of these

136.   Victory Parade after VE Day.

137. Even after the war, tragedy strikes: a fire at Craven Park Road in August 1945. From a painting by Mr. E. Monk.

nerve-wracking bombs killed 13 people, and one casualty was saved by a blood transfusion while still trapped in the wreckage.

Hitler's terror warfare only strengthened everyone's resolution. The Council provided stronger and better street shelters.

The bombs grew bigger and more destructive and Willesden's civil defence was often called on by neighbouring boroughs to help in the endless work of rescuing bombed people. Just before the end of the war, two rockets fell in one night on Willesden. A wing of Wykeham School collapsed and some nearby council houses were shattered. Seven people in Aboyne Road were killed and 40 were seriously injured. The blast was so severe that houses and shops in Neasden Lane were damaged.

This was the price paid, set out in harsh statistics.

The bare figures cannot measure the damage to people' lives:

Air raid warnings	1,000+
Bombs dropped:	
High explosives and	
parachute mines	572
Flying bombs and rockets	19
Incendiaries	many thousands
Casualties:	
Killed	372
Injured	2,108
Homes:	
Destroyed	1,300
Severely damaged	6,500

Then, suddenly, and thankfully, the ghastly war was over.

Chapter 22

Reconstruction

The Post-War Temperament

In the twenty years from 1945, the changes that affected Britain were, of course, evident in Willesden. The railways became British Railways. The hospitals became part of the National Health Service. Electricity and gas were made part of national networks rather than municipal or local private companies.

The national economy went boom and bust. Even worse was the effect on Willesden's busy factories. 'Closed', 'Closed', 'Closed' was the repeated sign. A boom in office building virtually by-passed Willesden, leaving it even more dilapidated.

If Neasden was dominant at the time of the Roberts family in the 17th century and important enough for its name to be used in preference to Willesden in the 10th century and again as a railway station name in the 19th, its rise and fall had led to the name becoming a 20th-century standing joke. *Private Eye* magazine made it its butt; Spike Milligan and Peter Cook used Neasden for further comic purposes. William Rushton, however, opening Neasden High School, said: 'Look out world, Neasden is on its way'. Ironically, the school closed some years later, but the local history museum in the Grange at Neasden has given the district the chance of a new image.

For about a dozen years from the 1950s to the '60s there was a series of major new large-scale immigrations, this time from the West Indies, East Africa and the Indian sub-continent. The new arrivals, many of them in fact refugees from oppression, aroused a wave of race hostility and conflict leading to repressive immigration laws. Yet, despite these sometimes open tensions, much was done to ease the pressures, for example, through the pioneering work of the Willesden International Friendship Council (now the Brent Community Relations Council). The abiding atmosphere was of tolerance in the localities. This did not prevent a deep-rooted wariness by the ethnic communities of the 'host' community but, equally, efforts were made by churches, by educationalists and by a wide range of people of goodwill to understand different cultures, recognise their value and urge their mutual acceptance.

A New Housing Drive

Willesden council set up sub-committees to look into the planning and development of the post-war community. The schemes generated much goodwill but bore no relation to post-war actuality.

In early 1945, the Mayor of Willesden, Jack Clark, called several municipal conferences and invited those interested in discussing plans for the future to attend. It was hoped to re-awaken the civic spirit and bring town hall and the people together.

Housing continued to exercise the energies and minds of the Willesden council for the post-war period until its absorption by Brent. Willesden's housing stock immediately after the war was about 38,000. The council provided 499 temporary bungalows and rebuilt war-destroyed houses—578 (mostly private houses)—some work not being completed until 1954.

The pace of new building was rather slow, partly because of the great need to repair war-damaged houses as well as rebuilding those destroyed. Also, the available land was less than in other parts of built-up London and, what there was, not so readily attainable. Willesden's need was much more in the field of redeveloping unsatisfactory 19th-century housing.

A review carried out in 1947-48, published as *The Willesden Survey 1949*, was a remarkable report and one still worth studying. The size of the problem facing Willesden's planners was revealed. Less than half the families had a bathroom to themselves; a quarter shared a lavatory. Housing densities varied from under 30 persons per acre or less than 0.7 persons per habitable room in parts of Brondesbury to over 150 persons per acre, over 1.3 persons per room, in South Kilburn and in Rucklidge Avenue. A decade later, when Brent was formed, and despite the great efforts of Willesden council, these were among

138. Post-war South Kilburn—as it might have been. From the *Willesden Survey* of 1949.

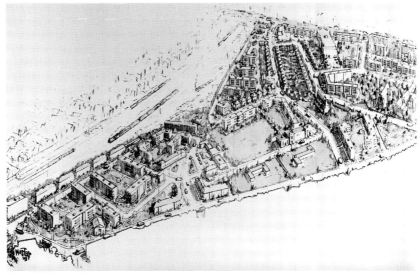

139. South Kilburn—as it became.

the problems inherited by the new local authority.

A development scheme for South Kilburn (north of Carlton Vale) had, in fact, been prepared in 1948 under the 1946 Housing Act, before the survey was published. It paved the way for the transformation of the area (which took about thirty years to complete). The layout that has emerged is very different from that originally proposed—particularly with the inclusion of tall 'high-rise' blocks of flats in place of two-storey houses initially wanted by the council or even the three or four-storey buildings first built.

This redevelopment was facilitated by a number of bombed sites and by the sale to the council by the Ecclesiastical Commissioners of about seven hundred houses before the leases fell in—some twenty acres of properties out of eighty-seven. This gave the council greater leverage in controlling the nature of the changes. Yet time slipped by. The slums grew worse. By 1950 only two blocks had been built. Carlton House and Chichester House. The survey, however, covered more than the housing difficulties. Industry, shopping, transport, open space and community services—from hospitals to cinemas—were all reviewed. Standards were outlined, the existing facilities described and proposals put forward.

One feature of the post-war scene that started off with the highest of hopes was the New Towns policy. The survey included research into willingness or desire of residents to move to a New Town—Hemel Hempstead being particularly associated with Willesden. Not surprisingly, half of Willesden's population expressed a wish to move right away if housing and employment were available. Most of those willing to move were young people under 30 years of age. The older ones, and those in the more prosperous, better housed areas, preferred to stay put. The first to move to Hemel Hempstead was a bricklayer and his family and he would, in turn, help to build more houses for Willesden folk.

During the 20-year post-war drive (leaving aside the rebuilding of war-destroyed properties), in the first decade the local authority built about 400 houses and flats, private enterprise producing a similar quantity. In the second decade, up to the formation of Brent, Willesden provided nearly 1,300 houses and flats; private enterprise, hemmed in by lack of land, built 365.

With the 1957 Rent Act, more problems of eviction and homelessness arose and Willesden council did its best to help with mortgage schemes, with rehousing and by becoming the first council to support housing co-operatives.

Willesden picked on the American term 'senior citizens' to describe housing for retired people and built blocks like Ellerslie and Frontenac (named after former houses on those sites). Elsewhere old people's flats abounded, many within existing council estates, thus allowing the retired

140.   Willesden housing, tower blocks on Shoot-up-Hill.

people to remain in the community rather than be exiled to lonely outposts for the elderly. Tall blocks such as Watling Gardens, Summit Court and others on the site of decayed or war-damaged mansions in Shoot-up-Hill were part of the housing drive. Bernard Shaw House at the top of Hillside, Stonebridge, provided constant hot water, tiled bathrooms, a communal automatic laundry, sunken gardens and social rooms.

Public Events
The Olympic Games in 1948, the Festival of Britain in 1951, and the Coronation of Queen Elizabeth in 1953 were events of nationwide importance. In most localities there were reflections of the central theme.

Many of the Olympic Games took place in our neighbouring district, Wembley. The famous stadium was the main centre for athletics, hockey and show-jumping with some other sports at the Palace of Engineering and swimming at the Empire Pool. Some competitors were housed in local colleges and schools. Notable absentees were athletes from the USSR, from Germany and Japan.

The opening by King George V on 29 July 1948 was celebrated in traditional style with the lighting of the Olympic flame by the last in a relay of runners who had started from Greece, each bearing a flaming torch. These burned a solid wax fuel and bore the inscription

XIV OLYMPIAD. OLYMPIA TO LONDON
WITH THANKS TO THE BEARER

One of them is in the mayor's parlour in Brent Town Hall.

Willesden council organised, tentatively at first, the Willesden Show and a Willesden Arts Festival. The show took over from the hospital carnivals, when the introduction of the National Health service reduced the need for hospitals to survive on charitable donations. The redoubtable 'Bomber' Harris, the entertainments manager for the council, led the way in these fun-filled events.

The Festival of Britain was the Labour government's brave and, on the whole, successful attempt to raise the spirits of post-war Britain and show that 'Britain Can Make It'. Its most enduring legacy was the architectural stimulus initiated by the South Bank Exhibition. In Willesden a festival girl competition was held and the winner was Daphne Weston who also became carnival queen. There were street parties again. Concert parties gave pleasure to thousands in the Roundwood and Gladstone Summer Theatres. There was folk-dancing and performances of *A Midsummer Night's Dream*. Festival Relish was on sale at 1s. 3d. a

141.   Willesden carnival in 1948.

142.   Celebrating the Coronation in Willesden, 1953.

jar! A festival week was declared in September
with fireworks to illuminate the opening and a
shopping week to show off the goods now proudly
on display.

The Coronation of Queen Elizabeth II in 1953,
like the Silver Jubilee of King George 18 years
earlier and the Queen's own 25 silver jubilee in
1977, aroused the deepest patriotic and loyalist
instincts—as much, or more, in the working class
districts as anywhere. Willesden gave 4,000 older
citizens a gift food parcel, souvenirs for children
and an enlarged Bank Holiday carnival. Street
parties were very popular in many parts of both
boroughs. A Coronation regatta was held on the
Welsh Harp on 6 June.

Public Buildings
Willesden council made a determined effort to
secure public halls for popular use. Anson Hall,
once the site of St Gabriel's church and later the
parochial hall, was taken over in 1948 and given
its present name after a careful search for the
most appropriate one. It served the entertainments
department well since there was a lack of such
facilities. The Music and Drama Festival was held
there for many years and Saturday dances were
popular. Foresters' Hall in Kilburn High Road was
bought with the proceeds from the sale of the
electricity undertaking—pre-war it had been used
as a theatre and for socials and dances. It has now
become the home of the Tricycle Theatre
Company. Christ Church hall was also acquired
and renamed Mapesbury Hall. Brondesbury and
Kilburn Girls' School used it for their dramatic
offerings but later it was used for social events
and eventually was leased to a commercial
company.

In Willesden Jewish cemetery there is a Jewish
National War Memorial, erected by the
Commonwealth War Graves Commission and
dedicated to Jewish servicemen who fell in the
two World Wars and who have no known grave.
This cenotaph was unveiled by Field-Marshal Sir
Gerald Templar in March 1960.

In Gladstone Park a set of remarkable
sculptures was made by Fred Kormis (himself a
prisoner in both wars) who presented them to the
council. They depict human suffering and
deliverance and are a memorial to prisoners of
conscience. They were dedicated in 1969 by the
Mayor, Alderman A. W. Sharpe accompanied by
a friend of the sculptor, the M. P. Reg Freeson.
The dedication was acknowledged by a former
prisoner of war and member of Brent's staff, Mr.
F. T. Ryall.

143. Kormis statues in Gladstone Park, 1971.

Industry in Decline
The *Willesden Survey* of 1949 said that the location
of industries could be divided into, firstly,
industrial estates such as Park Royal, Church End
and North Cricklewood. Secondly, industrial pock-
ets such as Coombe Road, Neasden, South
Cricklewood (Smith's and Rolls Razor, etc.),
Lonsdale Road, Kilburn, Brentfield Road, and
Stonebridge. Thirdly there was, and still is,
scattered or non-conforming industry, to repeat
the ugly jargon, in almost every area except
Brondesbury and Dollis Hill.

In 1949 half Willesden's industrial activities
were carried on in pre-1913 premises even though
90 per cent of the industries were of post-1918
origin. The explanation lay partly in the
disappearance of the old smaller firms, partly the
surge of activity in the 1920s and '30s and lastly
in the fact that many small industries and workshops were in stables, coach-yards and so on,
converted from their erstwhile purpose (for

144. Industry closing down—Rolls Razors, Cricklewood in the 1960s.

example, Lonsdale Road, Kilburn. Just one example is the coach-building firm, Hoopers, who provide bodywork for Rolls Royce and Bentley cars, having moved there from North Wembley, after the First World War).

The ten years from the mid-1960s saw an acceleration of a process begun earlier—a reduction in manufacturing capacity in Willesden (as elsewhere in the country), an increase in service industries, including warehousing, and an overall decline in the number of jobs available in the borough.

The Office Boom

Office development in the 1960s provoked a reaction that was a protest against this manifestation of the 'affluent society' with a critical shortage of decent homes in the shadow of these same offices. Two-and-a-half million square feet of office floor area was approved in Brent,

between 1956 and 1966, although this was mostly located in Wembley.

It is an interesting reflection on the trend in late 20th-century employment that the *Willesden Survey* of 1949 devoted no special mention to office employment (other than as part of local government which then, as now, was the biggest single employer of all types of labour).

Station House, at the junction of the Harrow and North Circular Roads, close by Stonebridge Park station, overshadows a corner of Willesden and the building and also the converted bus garage now known as Bridge Park. Station House was 'topped out' by the first Mayor of Brent, John Hockey.

Other office blocks found their way into the hands of government departments including Chancel House on the site of the former BTH/AEI site in Neasden Lane opposite St Mary's church.

Chapter 23

Enter Brent

On 31 March 1965 Willesden, as a local government entity, 'died' and Brent was born. The new era brought with it some of the longer-lasting changes associated with the 'Swinging Sixties' (one very short-lived fashion was the display in a Willesden High Road shop of topless dresses—outraged citizens soon obtained a 'cover up').

The physical shape of Willesden was changing—not simply its boundaries as part of the newly-created borough but through the erection of tall blocks of flats (called 'high rise' in the jargon of the day) which were a hasty response to the pressures to overcome housing shortages.

The idea of redeveloping large sectors of apparently decayed Victorian inner cities (slums in 1930s terms) led to the razing of South Kilburn, followed by wholesale rebuilding in Stonebridge and Church End. Much of what was built firstly by Willesden, and then by Brent, was in the form of tower blocks (except, fortunately, in Church End which was developed into maisonnettes and in Kensal Green, where wholesale redevelopment was prevented by local opinion in favour of renovation).

The name of the river which had previously separated Willesden from its westerly neighbour was chosen for the new borough and Brent emerged ready for the tasks ahead.

At the first meeting of the new council on 25 May 1964 the last Mayor of Wembley, Councillor Gornall, took the chair for the election of the first chairman of the new borough (during the initial year, the new councils were presided over by a chairman and not a mayor). The council then elected, without dissent, Willesden councillor and its former Leader, Reg Freeson, shortly to become one of Brent's M.P.s and also a Brent Alderman.

Wembley Town Hall was evidently more centrally located within the new borough than Willesden's which was on the edge of its original district. The old Victorian building was used as local offices for a time but eventually the decision was taken—with mixed feelings—that its continued use could not be justified.

The Borough's motto *Forward Together* contains an image of both the past and the 'yet-to-come'.

Simeon Potter said in the concluding chapter of the *Story of Willesden* in 1926:

It is not so easy for us to know all the important things about our parish as it was for the villagers of old. But if we are to win for ourselves and others a noble civic spirit, we must not be content to think, but we must strive to know. We must know yet more about

145. Stonebridge Park, Phase 2, 1967.

126

146. *(Above)* Brent Mayor John Hockey opening Ryde House in January 1966, in honour of a former Mayor of Willesden.

147. *(Right)* Brent Coat of Arms.

the past, so that the things which are valuable and worthy of memory may not die and be forgotten, but may be made useful again. The more we know about our own parish, the better equipped we are for that great struggle which lies before us, stretching onwards and upwards into the future, the struggle against poverty, ignorance and disease.

The Willesden Story by Leff and Blunden 40 years later concluded:

A new view—So this was the Willesden story. Seen over a long distance, back to the days of the "hill with a spring", and the first groping attempts of people to make some order in their lives, it was a story of effort and change.

Sometimes the change was gradual and hardly noticed by people following the unexciting routine of their days. Sometimes there was a deep impact, and people knew that life in Willesden would never be quite the same again. But there were always some things which remained the same for each generation: the need for and the love of home; the friendliness of familiar street names; the reassuring presence of the parish church, the vestry, or the town hall.

Before there was a place called Brent, there was Willesden, with its busy high streets, blocks of flats and rows of houses, libraries and schools, parks and playgrounds—all the familiar places where people lived,

experienced changes and enjoyed a measure of security. Nothing of that would change, except to be carried forward into the future.

A writer in 1927 tried to visualise the Willesden of 1977 (he could not forecast the merger with Wembley but made some surprisingly accurate guesses).

The writer concluded:

The control of certain essential services by the municipality will by no means kill private enterprise which will be fostered and encouraged. No more calamitous strikes will hamper and hold up our industries. We shall be living in a more enlightened age and a happier and more contented people will devise better means of settling industrial problems. Class hatred will be a thing of the past; it will be an age of ample opportunities for all and all positions will be available to those who qualify to fill them. For the rest, life will go on ... human nature will be pretty much what it has always been.

(From the *Willesden Chronicle* 50th Jubilee edition.)

It may not quite have worked out like that— though how much of the prediction came true— but for the future of Willesden, now part of Brent, one thing is true—it will be interesting, going Forward Together. Long Live Willesden!

Index

Numbers in **bold** refer to illustrations (page numbers)